The
Collected
Poems of
Robert Creeley

1945 • 1975

THE
COLLECTED
POEMS OF
Robert Creeley

1945 • 1975

UNIVERSITY OF CALIFORNIA PRESS
Berkeley
Los Angeles

For Love: Poems, 1950–1960 is copyright © 1962 by Robert Creeley (New York: Charles Scribner's Sons, 1962) and *Pieces* is copyright © 1969 by Robert Creeley (New York: Charles Scribner's Sons, 1969); both are reprinted with the permission of Charles Scribner's Sons.

Grateful acknowledgment is made to the publishers of the other collections reprinted in this volume: *Words* (New York: Charles Scribner's Sons, 1967); *In London*, from *A Day Book* (New York: Charles Scribner's Sons, 1972); *His Idea* (Toronto: Coach House Press, 1973); *Thirty Things* (Santa Barbara, Calif.: Black Sparrow Press, 1974); *Backwards* (Knotting, Bedfordshire: The Sceptre Press, 1975); *Away* (Santa Barbara, Calif.: Black Sparrow Press, 1976); and *The Charm* (San Francisco: Four Seasons Foundation, 1979). The author also gives thanks to the publishers of the broadsides and journals in which the poems gathered for the first time in this book originally appeared: *Journal of Creative Behavior*, Indianakatz Production, Black Sparrow Press, *Stone Drum*, *Fire Exit*, *Paintbrush*, *Paris Review*, Lodestar Press, *Beau Fleuve*, and *Just Buffalo*.

811.5
C

University of California Press
Berkeley and Los Angeles, California

© 1982 by
The Regents of the University of California

Distributed throughout Europe and the Commonwealth (except Canada) by Marion Boyars Publishers Ltd., 18 Brewer Street, London W1R 4AS

Library of Congress Cataloging in Publication Data
Creeley, Robert, 1926–
    The collected poems of Robert Creeley, 1945–1975.

    Includes index.
    I. Title.
PS3505.R43A17   1982   811'.54   81-19668
ISBN 0-520-04243-3   AACR2
ISBN 0-520-04244-1 (pbk.)

Printed in the United States of America
1 2 3 4 5 6 7 8 9

Grief, grief I suppose and sufficient
Grief makes us free
To be faithless and faithful together
As we have to be.

D. H. LAWRENCE
Hymn to Priapus

Contents

THERE IS A SENSE OF INCREMENT, of accumulation, in these poems that is very dear to me. Like it or not, it outwits whatever I then thought to say and gains thereby whatever I was in saying it. Thankfully, I was never what I thought I was, certainly never enough.

Otherwise, when it came time to think specifically of this collection and of what might be decorously omitted, I decided to stick with my initial judgments, book by tender book, because these were the occasions most definitive of what the poems might mean, either to me or to anyone else. To define their value in hindsight would be to miss the factual life they had either made manifest or engendered. So everything that was printed in a book between the dates of 1945 and 1975 is here included as are also those poems published in magazines or broadsides. In short, all that was in print is here.

I'm delighted that they are all finally together, respected, included, each with their place—like some ultimate family reunion! I feel much relieved to see them now as a company at last.

I'm tempted to invoke again those poets who served as a measure and resource for me all my life as a poet. But either they will be heard here, in the words and rhythms themselves, or one will simply know them. This time I am, in this respect, alone and these are my poems. We are a singular compact.

However, I thank very gratefully the several people who are in large part responsible for this particular book, most especially Carroll Terrell, whose idea it first was; Tim Murray, who undertook the laborious recovery of fugitive publications; and Marilyn Schwartz, who held the proverbial hand.

Finally, there's no end to any of it, or none we'll know that simply. But I'm very relieved that this much, like they say, is done. So be it.

Robert Creeley

Wilmington, N.C.
June 29, 1981

N.B. Insofar as the specific lines of these various poems are, in each case, the defining rhythmic unit, it is crucial that their integrity be recognized, else a false presumption of a poem's underlying beat may well occur in those cases where a runover line, i.e., a line broken by the limits of a page's dimensions, may be mistaken for the author's intent. Therefore all such lines are preceded by this symbol (◁) and are indented the characteristic space (1 em) from the poem's left margin. Read them as if they were one with the lines which they follow.

R.C.

The Charm

The poems in this book begin at the very beginning so to speak—"Return" was the first poem I remember having published, and was written on my coming back from India to Cambridge in the winter of 1945—and continue to a time which would include the writing of many of the poems in *Words*. Why there are this number, I don't altogether know. When *For Love* was first a possibility, I lacked copies of many of the earlier small books I had published, and had none of the manuscripts, so that I was dependent on texts such as *The Whip* (effectually a *selected poems*) and *A Form of Women*. Consequently I depended on the poems I had literally in hand and could not reconsider others I had cut from previous collections for whatever reason.

However, one poem—the title poem of this book, first published in *The Kind of Act of* in 1954—continued to stick in my head for many years indeed. The 'tongue' of that poem is still the one I am given to speak with. More I *like* this poem—in that it has continued to speak both for and to me, for all that time.

When I first began writing, I was very didactic and very involved with 'doing it right.' There was so much then to qualify what was acceptably a poem, and what was not. For example, there is a lovely story told me by John Frederick Nims about a friend of his reading somewhere in the Midwest. At the end someone in the audience asked if questions were permitted, and being told they were, said that he had one concerning the next to last poem read—to wit, 'Was that a real poem or did you just make it up yourself?'

In any case, whenever there was a chance to publish a small pamphlet or book, my temptation was to cut from it any poem that did not seem to me then and there to make adamant sense as a *poem*, and consequently I tended to ignore a kind of statement in poetry that accumulates its occasion as much by means of its awkwardnesses as by its overt successes.

One time in conversation with Allen Ginsberg late at night, when we were both in Vancouver in 1963, he very generously said to me, you don't have to worry so much about writing a 'bad' poem. You can afford to now. I don't know that my nature will ever allow me that understanding, which has not finally to do with some pompous self-regard— but rather with the fact that we are human beings and do live in the variability of that order. We don't know all we think we do, nor would it even be very interesting if we did. Another friend, Robert Duncan, has always insisted, with high intelligence, I think, that poetry is not some ultimate preserve for the most rarified and articulate of human utter-ances, but has a place for *all* speech and *all* occasions thereof.

Let me be, then, as gullible as obviously I once must have been, and enjoy the fact of having written these poems— which I know I did then, just that to be given to write anything is always pleasure. Selfishly enough, I can often discover myself here in ways I can now enjoy having been— no matter they were 'good' or 'bad.'

1967

Return

Quiet as is proper for such places;
The street, subdued, half-snow, half-rain,
Endless, but ending in the darkened doors.
Inside, they who will be there always,
Quiet as is proper for such people—
Enough for now to be here, and
To know my door is one of these.

Greendoon's Song

it's the greyness said greendoon
bids the several of our clan
seek forever for a man
to put music in our tune

it's the brownness turns the leaf
sets us searching while we can
up and down the stranger land
for a single honest thief

it's the blackness of our grief
brings us back into the room
puts the lock into our hand

Poem for D. H. Lawrence

I would begin by explaining
that by reason of being
I am and no other.

Always the self returns to
self-consciousness, seeing
the figure drawn by the window
by its own hand, standing
alone and unwanted by others.
It sees this, the self sees
and returns to the figure
there in the evening, the darkness,
alone and unwanted by others.

In the beginning was this self,
perhaps, without the figure,
without consciousness of self
or figure or evening. In the
beginning was this self only,
alone and unwanted by others.

In the beginning was that and this
is different, is changed and how
it is changed is not known but felt.
It is felt by the self and the self
is feeling, is changed by feeling,
but not known, is changed, is felt.

Remembering the figure by the window,
in the evening drawn there by the window,
is to see the thing like money, is to be
sure of materials, but not to know
where they came from or how
they got there or when they came.
Remembering the figure by the window
the evening is remembered, the darkness
remembered as the figure by the window,
but is not to know how they came there.

The self is being, is in being and
because of it. The figure is not being
nor the self but is in the self and
in the being and because of them.

Always the self returns to, because of
being, the figure drawn by the window,
there in the evening, the darkness,
alone and unwanted by others.

Poem for Beginners

. . . and I could see in the clearing
beside the axe and the tree   (fallen)
I'd cut before dinner   (morning)
a squirrel and I ran for . . .   (problem)

So that one who has come back in passion
may sit by the other who has not left
and turn to this one and explain
what has happened and remain with it
unexplained; so that the other may sit
and return with this other in passion,
come back and remain unexplained;
so that each, together, may sit
and together each may, together, explain
and remain; it is, perhaps, necessary to complain
that it is passion which does this, does not explain.

—If you will follow this road as far as
the turning, you will come to a barn
with a red roof and a large silo.
If you ask them there, they should know
(i.e. they'll tell you where you want to go.)

Because, more than anything, it is the road
and its turnings that is the traveler,
that comes back and remains unexplained
and even sits in the doorway and looks over
the hills and sees sunsets and calls you
to see them too; because it is the road
that the returned one has traveled who
travels, who goes and comes and remains;
perhaps it is the road who can, perhaps, explain
that it is the passion which does this, does not complain.

—She was coming over before breakfast
to tell you herself but then she remembered
she'd told Judy and all the rest
of them that she was going to make bread

(because she didn't believe what he'd said
until the morning and the somehow unfamiliar bed.)

If, then, the problem is the road
and the passion we call traveler and one
who has remained; if it is to blame one
for coming or going, remaining or staying the same
or, perhaps, for not explaining or, better,
for not complaining; is there a name
for it? What is there, after all, to explain?
That passion is wild, the road runs, the traveler
has come back and sits and talks and goes again?
Perhaps it is the road and passion which complain
that it is the traveler who does this, does not explain.

. . . and I could see in the clearing
beside the axe and the tree   (fallen)
I'd cut before dinner   (morning)
a squirrel and I ran for my gun.

Sanine to Leda

Beyond this road the blackness bends
in warmth. Two, then three or four,
lovers with wisdom for themselves
enough are sitting there in vague,
unbending poses. They sit.
The quiet grass holds roses.

Begin with that. The beautiful
comes later. Love, the several roses,
lovers with wisdom for themselves,
vague, unbending poses. Look.
Each loses what he chooses.

The Late Comer

(parvenue) delinquent, who will now
guess that this, that this is you,
as if a delinquent, a late sorrow
had arranged this, being better
this way, being better late than

never,

for (believe me) there are still
flowers there, though wilted, there
are still flowers, as if there are
their flowers and wilted, their
sorrow, delinquent, as if in cool

weather.

It was never this or that they
wanted, so given their sorrow, or
was what they wanted yours and
would you have given them over
the flowers, the coolness, delinquent . . .

(better)

Gangster

he said, turning, unconscious of
emphasis, why—goddamn it—I
was almost a gangster! Could
shoot straight. That's it. So
at morning, coming alone and
walking five miles, he could see
the horns and waited. Looking.
Until it was all there. He fired.

Simple? How simple? To say what's
what takes how much? Three cans
in a row, from the hip yet. No
joke. But to worry, to think
of it that way (the gangster)—
to see yourself like others
see you, Jesus, what pride!

Quieter, a wife and two children,
he'll wait for a reckoning.

Poem for Bob Leed

O and we sang then whose voices
loud long-echoed so that the many
trees could not surround them and
we sang the warm songs the graceful
expositions the particular songs
and O the woods echoed what we sang

It is the long road he is coming
where dust all day rises and the sun
at noon is darkened with dust and in
the dry mouth the water is brittle,
tasteless. It is the day he lives
and the long road, dust-driven, no
stranger but who's all alone here
where he is, is coming tomorrow.

From windows, fresh curtains which smell
good and the hand that holds them there's
a stranger but none who could know it
and whose house is, what house is, now
a question, whose and tomorrow's
a day of dust and the road is another's.

What would it now take, another, a question
like others to answer, what now could
take him in, one bed for a stranger, long-
limbed and once handsome, who's ready to try
for the particular, adequate lover? Tomorrow
he'll die and be dead and whose bed will be
empty? One word, whose word, could be said.

but O and we sang then whose voices

From Pico & the Women: A Life

Love God, we rather may, than
either know Him, or by speech
utter him . . . Disuse, good father,

these things have rusted and
we know a man who speaks more
freely of these and other, of

all wonders. We have hands,
now, and can hold all wonders.
And yet had men liefer, good

father, *by knowledge never find*,
good father, *that which they*
seek . . . These words are twisted.

     •

Today is a green day. Today
we are away from those involving
questions, that the gods have

put upon us, wittingly, to bind,
to fetter, and surprise. And
the god's eye is clear, is an

unsurprising blue, with which
we are each familiar. We are
born to blue, under, god's lid,

good sky, blue sky, with which
we are each familiar. We are
born to sky, under, god's eye.

     •

He will be sleeping somewhere
else, little rabbit, in the long
grass, in the hole of his own

making. He will be sleeping and
it will be our fear that lies
so. It is not our time nor our

spirit, but we will come to it.
It is our lion of fire, our
triumphant animal, with his own

victories, our hearts' conquesting
beast, little rabbit, that will
not bite you nor otherwise harm.

To the One in the Gray Coat

To the one in the gray coat,
sitting as though he were
asleep, were beyond these
involving actions, I will
address myself. Olé!

He will become conscious,
so, of the south. I have
called to mind for him,
have suggested by language,
a world of inner warmth,

a south of the spirit in
which he will be the one
who is not asleep, who
dozes in the completeness
of things which are warm,

in the sun, in the sun's
completeness. And the coat
as remnant, to be left on
the bench. And he will
know this and will leave it.

Then, going, he will have
passed me, in chill air,
the disciple, to say more
of, to go on with these
signs of inadequate love.

The Epic Expands

They had come in a carriage (which
will be less than what's needed)
over the hard roads. And they stop
in the town to get coke, three
bottles, by way of a celebration.

So will the epic expand (or be
expanded by) its content. So will
words throw (throw up) their meaning.
Words they have used (will use) are
the sound (of sound), what gets us.

But to go farther (he could not
stop there), to look at the old
people, graceless and cold, in a
carriage with only one blanket
between them, to keep out the cold—

and it was, he said (he said), it
was a coldness of the mind, too (too).
Yes, poets, we had overlooked an
essence, and quiet (put back into
quiet), we let the tears roll down.

Love

The thing comes
of itself
      (Look up
to see
     the cat & the squirrel,
               the one
torn, a red thing,
         & the other
somehow immaculate

Still Life Or

mobiles:
        that the wind can catch at,
against itself,
          a leaf or a contrivance of wires,
in the stairwell,
to be looked at from below.

We have arranged the form of a formula here,
have taken the heart out
            & the wind
is vague emotion.

To count on these aspirants
these contenders for the to-be-looked-at part
of these actions
        these most hopeful movements
needs
a strong & constant wind.
          That will not rise above the speed
which we have calculated,
        that the leaf
remain
     that the wires
be not too much shaken.

Hélas

Hélas! Or Christus fails.
The day is the indefinite. The shapes of light
have surrounded the senses,
but will not take them to hand (as would an axe-edge
take to its stone . . .)

It is not a simple bitterness that comes between.
Worn by these simplicities, the head
revolves, turns in the wind but lacks
its delight.

What, now, more than sight
or sound could compel it, drive, new,
these mechanics for compulsion

                    (nothing else but
to bite home! there, where
the head could take hold . . .)

                       which are vague,
in the wind,
take no edge from the wind, no edge
or delight?

Guido, i' vorrei che
tu e Lapo ed io

Guido,
I would that you, me & Lapo
                              (so a song sung:
                              sempre d'amore . . .)
were out of this
                    had got to the reaches
of some other wood.

Deadness
            is echo
deadness is memory
                        & their deadness is
petulant, the song gone
dead in their heads.

Echo
        is memory
and all that they foster
                            is dead in its sound
has no ripeness
could come to its own.

Petulance
            is force so contested.
They have twisted
                    the meanings & manner
the force of us out of us
left us the faded
                    (Who made musick
the sound of the reaches
                            the actual wood

Hart Crane 2

Answer: how old
is the wind, shakes the trees & moves with the movement of
(what is
          sound

I am again, and no more than
it was
         when the wind, when the trees, what
(is the sound of
            sound

(Sd he: the miracle
is it not, in our bath
like a lump of sugar
we don't dissolve
             (makes incorporeal even
their lightest phrase)

So sound is, was (apocryphal) the sound of
sound
      (what love
            apolaustic
                  had broke this thing

Littleton, N.H.

Day/
    diminutive

Night is the Mother, is the
Fixer of Change.

From which, from out of which
the Mind can take its center.

                        The Moon
as, say, round & inconsequent (Shine on

They say here, that, for change: the (4)
quarters of this most luminous moon
(now) must each be taken. Like
(not to be laughed at) the quarters
of a pie (or where the dollar goes . . .), it is
the graph, the locus of change.

Impossible (it is) for the stranger
to ever get these facts. He wanders alone here,
finds drift & satisfaction equally off & away from him.
There was that road
turned off from the main one
to end in the backyard.

Now, (sua culpa) Kenneth stands in the corner
and remarks the cloud drift from
the third corner of
                        (not the room but) life.
His moon is the shade of the moon in the corner
of his room
                (where it makes: the Sign

Canzone

as would any sound make
more music
                        than this scraping
his violin is not love
is not even love lacking
a purpose or an object for
its love

                (is not even sound
since sound has a shape in
the ear and this has no shape)

or
him & his violin

Love

Not enough. The question: what is.
Given: grace
          the time of this moment
which I do not see as time.
The particulars: oak, the grain of, oak.
And what supple shadows may come
to be here.

Tell me something I don't know.
Of love, and I hear it, say:
speak to me, of love . . .
                    The crouched hand.
The indefatigable.
                    But quicken, but be
the quick!

. . . *the stain of love is upon the world!*

Which I have not written.

The Festival

Death makes his
obeisance:
   to the two
first, children. The wall
falling, to catch them and then
another, the aunt aged 6
also.

The Surf: An Elegy

Relative to cost, the high figures
of production:
                      you, sweetness & light
are destructive only in your
inveterate tendencies.

The poor are poor. The statement
the little people would not
I think
accept, is

that there is any refuge
that there is anything to be gained
in too simple formulation.

Or what else to destroy them with?
To keep them you, lover
grant is impossible:
                      the blot
is nationwide, the indulgence
federal.
              Dams, projects of even
immense size
take on but
a few.
              (But you are restless, the tide
pulls out, leaving scum, the likewise restless
and improbable
stores of the sea.

The Drums

how are you harry the
last time we met it was
in heaven
surely
or so I remember

The Sea

the wash, the plunge
down
       (saying:
we will not become you, we
are the impenitents
                   (the tears

We declare

The Cantos

To make peace (borso
with the others,—or not too
quickly, give in to the companionable
ecstasy.

And she said, madame
your child speaks
french, whereas
previously
he could only hear it & we thought
understand.

A triumph. But dwindles quickly.
Since last fall he spoke it, I
had already
been proud, but not to her
of whom he had been frightened.

What to think of the dullness
of the provincial lady?
Not to think of it, we make
no makeshift adjustments
to the inadequacy
of anyone.

Something for Easter

I pulled the street up as you suggested
—and found what?

$\qquad$ 1 nickel
$\qquad$ 2 pieces gum

etc.

But we are practical
—but winter is long & however much one
does save, there is never
enough.

Divisions

1

Order. Order. The bottle contains
more than water. In this case the form
is imposed.

As if the air did not hold me in
and not let me burst from what have you or inveterate
goodwill!

To make it difficult, to make a sense
of limit, to call a stop to meandering—
one could wander here

in intricacies, unbelted, somewhat sloppy.
But the questions are, is it all there
or on some one evening

will I come again here, most desperate and all questions,
to find the water all
leaked out.

2

Take it, there are particulars.
Or consider rock. Consider hardness not as elemental but as
stone. The stone! And just so
invincible.

Which is to say, not a damn thing but
rock. But, just so, that hardness, which is to say:
the stone.

Or if only to consider, don't.
Loss exists not as perpetual but, exact, when the attentions
are cajoled,
are flattered by their purport or what they purport
to attend.

Which remains not, also not, definition.
But statement. But, very simply, one, just so, not
attend to
the business not
his own.

The Question

A description of the sensuous
is its own answer: a multiple love is
mine.
        These women.

Who in their beds, their
beds or buttocks bared for the nocturnal
revels, agh!

Or if her tits be rose, or roses, or any
flower, with what, say, to water this
garden of particular
intent?

A Poem

If the water forms
the forms of the weeds, there—

a long life is not by that
a necessarily happy one.

My friend. We
reckon on a simple

agreement,
the fashion of a stone

underground.

The Mirror

When I see you in the first light, again
at the angle of the bed, in a light seen

face, and hand, hair. The horrible
incompetence, and dull passive greyness
of myself.
           In disuse, and there is no use
got by nothing, and no competence
enough to make enough—

It becomes the incredible in which I believe,
that any god is love.

A Variation

1

My son who is stranger
than he should be, outgrown
at five, the normal—

luck is against him!
Unfit for the upbringing he would otherwise
have got, I have no hopes for him.

I leave him alone.

I leave him to his own
devices, having pity not so much that he is
strange

but that I am him.

2

Myself, who am stranger
than I should be, outgrown
at two, the normal—

luck is against me.   Unfit
for the upbringing I would otherwise
have got, I have no hopes.

I leave him alone.

I leave him to his own
devices, having pity not so much for
myself, for why should that happen

but that he is me, as much as I am him.

Two Ways of Looking in a Mirror

At midnight the world is a mediate
perspective.
               And hence
to an immaculate
bed, the time of

passion,
flower of my mind. Consumptive
prayers keep us: the moon in its low chamber.

And about us, rayed out in a floral wall-
paper-like pattern, the

facts of our union. Bliss
is actual, as hard as
stone.

Medallion

Light, a form, a
shadow at the edge of the window, a

sullenness comes over me, un-
repentant.

What if the others don't care, what
is it you want
                    (Lacunae

"flesh
of another color, a

whiter hand, with narrow, arching
fingers

Old Song

Take off your clothes, love,
And come to me.

Soon will the sun be breaking
Over yon sea.

And all of our hairs be white, love,
For aught we do

And all our nights be one, love,
For all we knew.

In an Act of Pity

In an act of pity your hands
are quietly offered, and are held at arm's
length, because they would be gentle.

Because I am not gentle my voice
is harsh, and my hands likewise. Because
I have nothing for you, and am wrong.

So it is to be wrong. To be at a loss
and unhappy, which is this loss
of one's happiness, in one who had held it.

The Charm

My children are, to me,
what is uncommon: they are dumb
and speak with signs. Their hands

are nervous, and fit more for
hysteria, than goodwill or long
winterside conversation.

Where fire is, they are quieter
and sit, comforted. They were born
by their mother in hopelessness.

But in them I had been, at first,
tongue. If they speak,
I have myself, and love them.

The Bird, the Bird, the Bird

for Charles

With the spring flowers I likewise am.
And care for them. That they have odor.

We are too garrulous (Brugm. i. §638), we
talk not too much but too often.

And yet, how otherwise to oblige the
demon, who it is, there

implacable, but content.

A Ballad

We have a song for the death in her body
and if the night is long
or the blackness blacker,
then something is effected from us.

But if, without hope, there is crying
and a moaning, a retching,
and the time is horrible,
and she cries and tries to escape from us—

do we then sit down with petulance
and a show of hate, and not like her?

For an Anniversary

Where you dream of water
I have held a handful of sand.

My manners are unprepossessing.
I stand here awkward, and a long time.

I am mainly an idiot.
You are almost beautiful.

We will both be miserable
but no one is damned

Los Guitaristas

The music is a dance
for the ones who don't dance, it is

a wiggle, obscene, beginning with the
hips, and ascending forthwith

to the mind.

Thank You

o Kindness, Kindness. These virtues are
for you pleasure, such

a radiance
of smiles, such

redundant satisfaction.

I Am Held by My Fear of Death

I am held by my fear of death.
I am deadened with it.

The thing in my hand is impassive
and will not

give me time. It is gone
and again I am

useless, impotent,
and the hell is potent

though I will not give in to it.
There is nothing beyond it.

The Method of Actuality

                              the
mother (mother) unbent to give to
anyone.
                The young
The sudden & inconsequent. The gentle
stare. I see myself in long & uncombed hair

bedridden, sullen, and face to face, a face of hair.
My mother's son.

The Pedigree

Or if I will not rape
my own daughter
     "What will I do?"

What, of what occasion, is not so
necessary, we do not
      "witless"
perform it.

    Or me.
Who am of common stock.

It Is at Times

als kleine begrüßung auf unserem
alten kontinent die paar zeilen

Of them, undefined
repetitions, the
inactual

        Lost, or spared
by the inaccurate, there
miscounted

           As of those lists
(the names)
repeated, the names
lost

     (As of an evening, talking
lost in
reflections, the

golden bowl

The Europeans

Or me wanting another man's
wife, etc.
      History.
Unable to keep straight
generations.

Telling them all about
myself.

The Penitent

These, the unequalled, vicious
beyond even
love (who act on it, there pulled to
a variation

cruel even, but at least of
the senses

But upon that corpus
who is of that, flesh of

Or why else turn to it, pathetic
hopeless to avoid or caught even as were
the penitents, pants down.

Eros

Also the headache of
to do right by feeling
it don't matter, etc.

But otherwise it was one, or even two
the space of, felt

and one night I said to her, do you
and she didn't.

For Martin

In the narcotic and act
of omniscience

a gain, of the formal,
is possible.

Time is the pleasure.
Forget all the diversities & digressions.

Love tonight for the mind
and the body together. Be relentless

that our ugliness
be inhabited.

The Trap

On a theme fantastic, a light
aria, by some altogether monstrous woman in
black tights,

the heart revolves itself,
congests, and tired,
lies to itself

again tired. Fastens
on sentiment.

The Revelation

I thought that if I were broken enough
I would see the light
like at the end of a small tube, but approachable.

I thought chickens laid eggs
for a purpose.

For the reason expected, a form occurred more
blatant and impossible

to stop me.

An Obscene Poem

The girl in the bikini, my
wife, the lady—she sits on
the rocks, crouched
behind a jagged encumbrance.

Calamares, canalones—
the fisherman's daughter.
At night a dull movement
on the sands

and lightly at low tide
on the rocks
bland, undulant
she returns.

Chasing the Bird

The sun sets unevenly and the people
go to bed.

The night has a thousand eyes.
The clouds are low, overhead.

Every night it is a little bit
more difficult, a little

harder. My mind
to me a mangle is.

Hi There!

Look, love
　　　　　　　* * * * * *
　　　　　　(oo)
　　　　　　　　springs
from out the
　　　　　　　* * * * * *
　　　　　　(oo)
　　　　　　( )
　　　　　　　　surface of a pedestrian
fact, a new
　　　　　　　* * * * * *
　　　　　　(oo)
　　　　　　( )
　　　　　　(----)
　　　　　　　　day.

Sopa

That old black goober that I ate
for lunch. Something in the bowl it was,

at the edge, up-
ended. Like when one

cracks one
peanut, how ever

to throw it away how-
ever dusty?

The Changes

People don't act
like they act
in real life
in real life. They

are slower
and record the passive changes
of atmosphere.

Or change themselves
into green persian dogs
and birds.
                When you see one
you know the world is a contrivance.
It has proverbiality.
People are poor.

For Irving

At seventeen women were strange & forbidden phenomenons.
Today they leer at me from street corners. Yet

who is to say it,
that we have come to an agreement.

Aging, aging, even so there is some song, some
remote pulse,

an argument still visible, an
excuse for it.

Broken Back Blues

O yr facing reality now—
& yr in the same beat groove—
you try to get up—
& find you just can't moo-oove
                              (take it take it
uncle john
we can play it all nite long . . .

            I got them things in my head—
no sounds will ever solve
                              (heh heh heh, heh heh heh . . .)

So yr bent in yr middle—
yr face is on the floor—
they take a great big club—
& beat you out the doo-oor
                              (watch it watch it

mr man
we're going to get you if we can

            that I'm alive today, I want to say, I want to say—
that I'm alive today
                              (heh heh heh, heh heh heh . . .)

I havent got a nickle—
I havent got a dime—
I havent got a cent—
I dont have that kind of time
                              (all rite for you, friend
                              that's the most
                              we herewith
                              propose a toast:
It's a hopeless world.

The Happy Man

Who would love you
if you were not six

feet tall, a ruddy face, a
smiling face. You

would walk all night, all
night, and no one, no one

would look at you.

For Somebody's Marriage

All night in a thoughtful
mood, she

resigned herself to a
conclusion—heretofore

rejected. She
woke lonely,

she had
slept well, yet

because of it her
mind was clearer, less

defended—
though confident.

Stomping with Catullus

1

My love—my love says
she loves me.
And that she would never have
anyone but me.

Though what a woman tells
to a man who pushes her
should be written in wind and quickly
moving water.

2

My old lady says I'm it,
she says nobody else cd ever make it.

But what my old lady says when pushed to it,—
well, that don't make it.

3

My old lady is a goof at heart,
she tells me she loves me, we'll never part—

but what a goofed up chick will tell to a man
is best written in wind & water & sand.

4

Love & money & a barrel of mud,
my old man gives out for stud,

comes home late from his life of sin,
now what do you think I should tell to him?

5

We get crazy but we have fun,
life is short & life gets done,

time is now & that's the gig,
make it, don't just flip yr wig.

The Apology

I think to compose a sonnet
on ladies with no clothes. A

graciousness to them
of course.

For a Friend

You are the one man
coming down the street on

a bicycle. And love is a certainty
because it is sure of itself.

The alphabet is letters,
the muskrat was a childhood friend.

But love is eternal,
and pathetic equally.

The Total Parts of a World

The form of the grasses against
the water is reminiscent, a total reminiscence
of the water in motion

and love itself a siren, a total
image.

Who is more unhappy than I am.
The voice wails. We

listen in unhappiness,
in love.

Alba

Your tits are rosy in the dawn
albeit the smallness of them.
Your lips are red and bright with love
albeit I lie upon them.

And hence the grossness of the act
reverberating ever
reinstitutes the virgin ground
of body and of fever.

An Irishman's Lament
on the Approaching Winter

Hello to you, lady,
who will not stay with me.

And what will you do now for warmth
in a winter's storm . . .

A cold wind take
your mind from its mistake.

Now Then

When love is for-
bidden, it

is the most!
says Huggi Baba, an old

egyptian? Perhaps an
old man already at the time

of this pronouncement, when
love is forbidden.

Trees

What shall I do with my friends,
if they won't answer my letters—
or if I make a joke, would it be better
not to send it to them?

This morning, clutching a daffodilly,
I sang of what things I could,
I would do better if I could. What would
make it all less silly.

Tonight when the goddess invokes me
with her back to me, would it do
to kick her too? Or should I tell it to you,
so that she will respect me.

I think: poets live in a well,
from whence the screams issue,
a fearsome hole it is too,
a very hell.

"To Work Is to Contradict Contradictions, to Do Violence to Natural Violence . . ."

To consummate
the inconsummate, and make of it

the unending. Work,
work, work.

Six days of the week you shall work,
on the seventh you shall think about it.

'Mary, pass the potatoes' becomes
division of subject & object.

Work, work, work.
Get them yourself.

Thought is a process of work,
joy is an issue of work.

Not Again

Sometimes I am embarrassed
by the recurrence of that pronoun
which calls into question, rather into
prominence, my own face.

Of course I
am embarrassed, what else?
Like with the waiter with the tray on which
repose (only) his own hands.

Always—
SundayMondayTuesdayWednesdayThursdayFriday
  ◁ Saturday—
no matter where I look,
I am there.

It was a breeze and a seashell
brought in Venus—
but I can be here
without going anywhere.

So goodbye
until we meet again,
and when you come, walk right in.
It's I.

The Prejudice

There is a despair one comes to,
awkwardly, in never having known
apple-breasted women.

But that time was inapproachable
when I was younger
and now am older.

O is that destiny,
she said to me.

"You've Tried the World, Try Jesus"

We laughed when he sat down at the piano
and it melted all over him.
We laughed later at the stew
we ate him in.

We laughed on the way home.
At that point he was inside us.
But now we are crying
and God won't hide us.

For a Screaming Lady

Pumping away pumping away
now everyone is pumping away.

The blood is circulated through the body
by hope faith and charity.

Big bands are assembled on every street corner
no one is crying anymore.

Now likewise when you see me you can look at me
because I won't be.

The Picnic

for Ed and Helene

Ducks in the pond,
icecream & beer,
all remind me
of West Acton, Mass—

where I lived when young
in a large old house
with 14 rooms
and woods out back.

Last night I talked
to a friend & his wife
about loons & wildcats
and how to live on so much money per month.

Time we all went home,
or back,
to where it all was,
where it all was.

The Menu

"John and I have decided
we do not like Al Haig . . ."

(Julia Wasp)
with applesauce

and pork
where there is smoke

there is desire
where what is true

is always true
I wouldn't like him either.

In a Boat Shed

I waited too long,
I waited for you forever and ever:

the changing unchanging restlessness
of the signs they didn't put up

or down; the boxes of oranges,
rat poisons, barns, a sled with no runners,

snow, refreshments, pineapples;
the odor of burnt wood, cigarettes

neither one of us should smoke,
but do—

I waited for you.

Swinging down Central

No matter what color my pants are
you are all in it together!
I don't want to go home.
Let me out let me out let me out.

Saturday was payday.
I keep saying. Pay me today.
I want my money
and want it now.

This night is love
night saturday dreams of
tokens of farewell on to
another's surprise surprise.

I should have died when I was seven
or eight or ten.
I should have been dead then
to have lived so long.

Je vois dans le hasard
tous les biens que j'espère

When you said 'accidental'
I thought it was that you were formal
and sat down.
When I went home I did not
go home. You said
go to bed, and sleep, and later
everything will be clear.

It was a lovely morning yesterday
and I think things have at last happened which will not go away.

The Herd

Way out they are riding, it is an old
time's way to continue to succeed
in recorded passionate hoofbeats,
animals moving, men before and behind them.

The Door

Thump. Thump. The door
which never is knocked upon but cries,
for who sings, dies,
what goes, will go on.

Nathaniel Hawthorne

Hippety hoppety down
and there they are

heppel's wait's father
uncle jim is

stone face
is the legend.

The Dream

A lake in the head
wherein they put a boat,
two trousered men
with four legs between them.

The women
go in swimming
in the nude.
They blossom into lewd.

That light shut off,
he rolls over
and under,
begins to smother.

The Hands

Take the hands
off of
it and throw
them so that
they re-
occur, else-
where on
some other
woman.

The Passage

What waiting in the halls,
stamping on the stairs,
all the ghosts are here tonight
come from everywhere.

Yet one or two,
absent, make
themselves felt by that,
break the heart.

Oh did you know I love you?
Could you guess?
Do you have, for me,
any tenderness left?

I cry to hear them,
sad, sad voices.
Ladies and gentlemen
come and come again.

What's for Dinner

Only from the back
could I be seen clearly,
merely the fragment
into space hanging.

John jumped on Tuesday.
We had a date
but I was late, and he unduly
unruly.

Today my time come, I
am hung from this 7th story downtown window
to say hello
for the last time.

The Animal

Shaking the head from
side to side, arms
moving, hanging as the
sign of pride,

mouth
wide open
to eat the
red meat

in the jungle,
in the heat.
But I am
not animal,

move,
discontinuous, on
two remote
feet. Then

it spoke, then
hair grew, and eyes,
and I
forgot my-

self—oh
no, oh not
(they say)
this like

an animal
he eats, and looks
like an animal
at us. It

spoke. Who
said it
could not, who
did not know.

The Sentence

There is that in love
which, by the syntax of,
men find women and join
their bodies to their minds

—which wants so to acquire
a continuity, a place,
a demonstration that it must
be one's own sentence.

The Ear

He cannot move the furniture
through that small aperture, yet
expects it must serve
used with reserve.

To wit, the company that comes
runs to be first in,
arranges what it can
within the man,

who (poor fool) bulges
with secrets he never divulges.

The Skeleton

The element in which they live,
the shell going outward until
it never can end, formless,
seen on a clear night as stars,
the term of life given them
to come back to, down to,
and then to be in
themselves only, only skin.

The Lion and the Dog

Let who will think of what they will.
If the mind is made up, like an animal,
a lion to be suffered, a dog to pat,
action follows without conclusion

till all is stopped. The conclusion
is not variable, it is. From that
which was, then it, the lion if it is,
or dog, if it is, is not. It has

died to who thought of it, but comes
again there, to wherever that mind was,
or place, or circumstance being compound
of place, and time, now waiting but patient.

And all that is difficult, but difficult
not to think of, saying, lion, dog, thinking,
thinking patience, as an occasion of these,
but never having known them. But they come,

just as they came once, he thought, he
gave them each all that they were, lion,
but a word merely, and only a dog of sound.
All die equally. The mind is only there,

but here he is, thinking of them. They
are patient. What do they know? They know
nothing. They are not but as he thought.
But he knows nothing who thinks. They are.

The Story

The tall woman wants the tall story
and sees from the tower, and saw more.

The history of acts is the form they make
toward one another as like waves they break.

The mind is coincident to any of several impinging
impregnated incidents like tomatoes ripening

—And the joke the friend told, incidentally, "the
young man who will accompany playing his silver balls,"

Did play them with a silver sound—and she
looked down and saw the small town from the far-off shore,

And the waves breaking and making up the ground
that ran from town to tower and then to her mind and back
 ◁ again.

Two Times

1

It takes so long to look down,
the first time thinking it
would then and there either
shoot up or else drop off.

2

One hand on
the trigger one
hand on the hand.

A Fragment

On the street I am met with constant hostility
and I would have finally nothing else around me,
except my children who are trained to love
and whom I intend to leave as relics of my intentions.

For Love

Wherever it is one stumbles (to get to wherever) at least some way will exist, so to speak, as and when a man takes this or that step—for which, god bless him. Insofar as these poems are such places, always they were ones stumbled into: warmth for a night perhaps, the misdirected intention come right; and too, a sudden instance of love, and the being loved, wherewith a man also contrives a world (of his own mind).

It seems to me, now, that I know less of these poems than will a reader, at least the reader for whom—if I write for anyone—I have written. How much I should like to please! It is a constant concern.

That is, however, hopeful and pompous, and not altogether true. I write poems because it pleases me, very much—I think that is true. In any case, we live as we can, each day another—there is no use in counting. Nor more, say, to live than what there is, to live. I want the poem as close to this fact as I can bring it; or it, me.

1962

1

1950 • 1955

Hart Crane

for Slater Brown

1

He had been stuttering, by the edge
of the street, one foot still
on the sidewalk, and the other
in the gutter . . .

like a bird, say, wired to flight, the
wings, pinned to their motion, stuffed.

The words, several, and for each, several
senses.
                "It is very difficult to sum up
briefly . . ."
                        It always was.

(Slater, let me come home.
The letters have proved insufficient.
The mind cannot hang to them as it could
to the words.

There are ways beyond
what I have here to work with,
what my head cannot push to any kind
of conclusion.

But my own ineptness
cannot bring them to hand,
the particulars of those times
we had talked.)

"Men kill themselves because they are
afraid of death, he says . . ."

The push
                beyond and
into

2

Respect, they said he respected the
ones with the learning, lacking it
himself
        (Waldo Frank & his
6 languages)
                What had seemed
important
While Crane sailed to Mexico I was writing
(so that one betrayed
                  himself)

He slowed
          (without those friends to keep going, to
keep up), stopped
              dead and the head could not
go further
          without those friends

. . . And so it was I entered the broken world

Hart Crane.

        Hart

Le Fou

for Charles

who plots, then, the lines
talking, taking, always the beat from
the breath
               (moving slowly at first
the breath
               which is slow—

I mean, graces come slowly,
it is that way.

So slowly (they are waving
we are moving

               away from   (the trees
               the usual   (go by
which is slower than this, is

               (we are moving!

goodbye

A Song

for Ann

I had wanted a quiet testament
and I had wanted, among other things,
a song.
        That was to be
of a like monotony.
                (A grace

Simply. Very very quiet.
               A murmur of some lost
thrush, though I have never seen one.

Which was you then. Sitting
and so, at peace, so very much now this same quiet.

A song.

And of you the sign now, surely, of a gross
perpetuity
             (which is not reluctant, or if it is,
it is no longer important.

A song.

Which one sings, if he sings it,
with care.

The Crisis

Let me say (in anger) that since the day we were married
we have never had a towel
where anyone could find it,
the fact.
          Notwithstanding that I am not
simple to live with, not
my own judgement, but no
matter.
        There are other things:

to kiss you is not
to love you.
        Or not so simply.

Laughter releases rancor, the quality of mercy is not
strained.

For Rainer Gerhardt

Impossible, rightly, to define these
conditions of
friendship, the wandering & inexhaustible wish to
be of use, somehow
to be helpful

when it isn't simple,—wish
otherwise, convulsed, and leading
nowhere I can go.

What one knows, then, not
simple, convulsed, and feeling
(this night)
petulance of all conditions, not
wondered, not even
felt.

I have felt nothing, I have
felt that if it were simpler, and
being so, it were a matter only of
an incredible indifference
(to us)
they might say it all—

but not friends, the
acquaintances, but you,
Rainer. And likely there is
petulance in us
kept apart.

The Riddle

What it is, the literal size
incorporates.
                    The question
is a mute question. One is
too lonely, one wants
to stop there, at the edge of

conception. The woman

imperative, the man
lost in stern
thought:

give it form certainly,
the name and titles.

The Rites

(Hogpen, deciduous growth, etc.
making neither much dent
nor any feeling: the trees completely
or incompletely
attached to ground

During which time all the time sounds of an anterior
◁ conversation
and what are they talking
about

Cares mount. My own
certainly
as much as anyone else's.
      Between
each and every row of seats
put a table
and put on that
an ashtray

(Who don't know what I know
in what proportion, is either off, too much
or on.

   Look it up, check
or if that's too much, say, too time-consuming or whatever
◁ other
neat adjective to attach to any
distraction
      (for doing nothing at all.

The rites are care, the natures
less simple, the mark of hell knows what but
something, the trace of

line, trace of
line made by someone

Ultimate: no man shall go unattended.
No man shall be an idiot for purely exterior reasons.

The Rhyme

There is the sign of
the flower—
to borrow the theme.

But what or where to recover
what is not love
too simply.

I saw her
and behind her there were
flowers, and behind them
nothing.

The Innocence

Looking to the sea, it is a line
of unbroken mountains.

It is the sky.
It is the ground. There
we live, on it.

It is a mist
now tangent to another
quiet. Here the leaves
come, there
is the rock in evidence

or evidence.
What I come to do
is partial, partially kept.

The Ball Game

The one damn time (7th inning)
standing up to get a hot dog someone spills
mustard all over me.

                       The conception is
the hit, whacko!
Likewise out of the park

of our own indifferent vulgarity, not
mind you, that one repents even the most visual
satisfaction.

Early in life the line is straight
made straight
against the grain.

Take the case of myself, and why not
since these particulars need
no further impetus

                    take me at the age of 13
and for some reason there, no matter the particular
reason.

        The one damn time (7th inning)
standing up to get a hot dog someone spills
mustard all over me.

The Carnival

Whereas the man who hits
the gong dis-
proves it, in all its
simplicity—

           Even so the attempt
makes for triumph, in
another man.

Likewise in love I
am not foolish or in-
competent. My method is not a

tenderness, but hope
defined.

After Lorca

for M. Marti

The church is a business, and the rich
are the business men.
                    When they pull on the bells, the
poor come piling in and when a poor man dies, he has a
   ◁ wooden
cross, and they rush through the ceremony.

But when a rich man dies, they
drag out the Sacrament
and a golden Cross, and go *doucement*, *doucement*
to the cemetery.

And the poor love it
and think it's crazy.

The Kind of Act Of

Giving oneself to the dentist or doctor who is a good one,
to take the complete
possession of mind, there is no

giving. The mind
beside the act of any dispossession is

lecherous. There is no more giving in
when there is no more sin.

The Dishonest Mailmen

They are taking all my letters, and they
put them into a fire.

                         I see the flames, etc.
But do not care, etc.

They burn everything I have, or what little
I have. I don't care, etc.

The poem supreme, addressed to
emptiness—this is the courage

necessary. This is something
quite different.

The Crow

The crow in the cage in the dining-room
hates me, because I will not feed him.

And I have left nothing behind in leaving
because I killed him.

And because I hit him over the head with a stick
there is nothing I laugh at.

Sickness is the hatred of a repentance
knowing there is nothing he wants.

The Immoral Proposition

If you never do anything for anyone else
you are spared the tragedy of human relation-

ships. If quietly and like another time
there is the passage of an unexpected thing:

to look at it is more
than it was. God knows

nothing is competent nothing is
all there is. The unsure

egoist is not
good for himself.

For W.C.W.

The pleasure of the wit sustains
a vague aroma

The fox-glove (unseen) the
wild flower

To the hands come
many things. In time of trouble

a wild exultation.

Apple Uppfle

Vanity (like a belly
dancer's romance): just
the hope. The unafraid & naked

wish, helpless. Pushed against a
huge & unending door . . .

And while the mind
a little more tenuous, more careful of it,
crabwise, gives in . . .

To the pleasure of a meal in silence.

The Operation

By Saturday I said you would be better on Sunday.
The insistence was a part of a reconciliation.

Your eyes bulged, the grey
light hung on you, you were hideous.

My involvement is just an old
habitual relationship.

Cruel, cruel to describe
what there is no reason to describe.

Chanson

Oh, le petit rondelay!
Gently, gently.
It is that I grow older.

As when for a lark
gaily, one hoists up a window
shut many years.

Does the lady's eye grow moist-
er, is it madame's in-
clination,

etc. Oh, le petit rondelay!
Gently, gently.
It is that I grow older.

Don't Sign Anything

Riding the horse as was my wont,
there was a bunch of cows in a field.

The horse
chased

them. I likewise, an uneasy
accompanist.

To wit, the Chinese proverb goes:
if you lie in a field

and fall asleep,
you will be found in a field

asleep.

The Conspiracy

You send me your poems,
I'll send you mine.

Things tend to awaken
even through random communication.

Let us suddenly
proclaim spring. And jeer

at the others,
all the others.

I will send a picture too
if you will send me one of you.

I Know a Man

As I sd to my
friend, because I am
always talking,—John, I

sd, which was not his
name, the darkness sur-
rounds us, what

can we do against
it, or else, shall we &
why not, buy a goddamn big car,

drive, he sd, for
christ's sake, look
out where yr going.

The End

When I know what people think of me
I am plunged into my loneliness. The grey

hat bought earlier sickens.
I have no purpose no longer distinguishable.

A feeling like being choked
enters my throat.

The Death of Venus

I dreamt her sensual proportions
had suffered sea-change,

that she was a porpoise, a
sea-beast rising lucid from the mist.

The sound of waves killed speech
but there were gestures—

of my own, it was to call her closer,
of hers, she snorted and filled her lungs with water,

then sank, to the bottom,
and looking down, clear it was, like crystal,

there I saw her.

The Lover

What should the young
man say, because he is buying
Modess? Should he

blush or not. Or
turn coyly, his head, to
one side, as if in

the exactitude of his emotion he
were not offended? Were
proud? Of what? To buy

a thing like that.

A Counterpoint

Let me be my own fool
of my own making, the sum of it

is equivocal.
One says of the drunken farmer:

leave him lay off it. And this is
the explanation.

Wait for Me

. . . give a man his
I said to her,

manliness: provide
what you want I

creature comfort
want only

for him and herself:
more so. You

preserve essential
think marriage is

hypocrisies—
everything?

in short, make a
Oh well,

home for herself.
I said.

The Business

To be in love is like going outside to see what kind of day

it is. Do not
mistake me. If you love

her how prove she
loves also, except that it

occurs, a remote chance on
which you stake

yourself? But barter for
the Indian was a means of sustenance.

There are records.

The Disappointment

Had you the eyes of a goat,
they would be almond, half-green, half-

yellow, an almond
shape to them. Were you

less as you are, cat-like, a brush
head, sad, sad, un-

goatlike.

The Warning

For love—I would
split open your head and put
a candle in
behind the eyes.

Love is dead in us
if we forget
the virtues of an amulet
and quick surprise.

A Form of Adaptation

My enemies came to get me,
among them a beautiful woman.

And—god, I thought, this will be the end of me,
because I have no resistance.

Taking their part against me even,
flattered that they were concerned,

I lay down before them and looked up soulfully,
thinking perhaps that might help.

And she bent over me to look at me then,
being a woman.

They are wise to send their strongest first, I thought.
And I kissed her.

And they watched her and both of us carefully,
not at all to be tricked.

But how account for love, even if you look for it?
I trusted it.

Song

Were I myself more blithe,
more the gay cavalier,
I would sit on a chair
and blow bubbles into the air.

I would tear up all the checks
made out to me,
not giving a good goddamn
what the hell happened.

I would marry a very rich woman
who had no use for stoves,
and send my present wife
all her old clothes.

And see my present children
on Mondays and Thursdays
and give them chocolate
to be nicer to me.

If being the word
as it was reported—
desperate perhaps, and even foolish,
but god knows useful.

Naughty Boy

When he brings home a whale
she laughs and says, that's not for real.

And if he won the Irish sweepstakes,
she would say, where were you last night?

Where are you now, for that matter? Am
I always (she says) to be looking

at you? She says,
if I thought it would get any better I

would shoot you, you
nut, you. Then pats her hair

into place, and waits
for Uncle Jim's deep-fired, all-fat, real gone

whale steaks.

Like They Say

Underneath the tree on some
soft grass I sat, I

watched two happy
woodpeckers be dis-

turbed by my presence. And
why not, I thought to

myself, why
not.

La Noche

In the court-
yard at midnight, at

midnight. The moon is
locked in itself, to

a man a
familiar thing.

The Whip

I spent a night turning in bed,
my love was a feather, a flat

sleeping thing. She was
very white

and quiet, and above us on
the roof, there was another woman I

also loved, had
addressed myself to in

a fit she
returned. That

encompasses it. But now I was
lonely, I yelled,

but what is that? Ugh,
she said, beside me, she put

her hand on
my back, for which act

I think to say this
wrongly.

All That Is Lovely in Men

Nothing for a dirty man
but soap in his bathtub, a

greasy hand, lover's
nuts

perhaps. Or else

something like sand
with which to scour him

for all
that is lovely in women.

2

1956 • 1958

Juggler's Thought

for my son, David

Heads up to the sky
people are walking by

in the land with no heads
tails hanging to trees

where truth is like an apple
reddened by frost and sun, and the green

fields go out and out
under the sun.

A Form of Women

I have come far enough
from where I was not before
to have seen the things
looking in at me through the open door

and have walked tonight
by myself
to see the moonlight
and see it as trees

and shapes more fearful
because I feared
what I did not know
but have wanted to know.

My face is my own, I thought.
But you have seen it
turn into a thousand years.
I watched you cry.

I could not touch you.
I wanted very much to
touch you
but could not.

If it is dark
when this is given to you,
have care for its content
when the moon shines.

My face is my own.
My hands are my own.
My mouth is my own
but I am not.

Moon, moon,
when you leave me alone
all the darkness is
an utter blackness,

a pit of fear,
a stench,
hands unreasonable
never to touch.

But I love you.
Do you love me.
What to say
when you see me.

They Say

Up and down
what falls
goes slower and slower
combing her hair.

She is the lovely stranger
who married the forest ranger,
the duck and the dog,
and never was seen again.

The Friend

What I saw in his head
was an inverted vision,
and the glass cracked
when I put my hand in.

My own head is round
with hair for adornment,
but the face
is an ornament.

Your face is wide
with long hair, and eyes
so wide they grow
deep as I watch.

If the world
could only be rounder,
like your head, like mine,
with your eyes for real lakes!

I sleep in myself.
That man was a friend,
sans canoe,
and I wanted to help him.

Please

for James Broughton

Oh god, let's go.
This is a poem for Kenneth Patchen.
Everywhere they are shooting people.
People people people people.
This is a poem for Allen Ginsberg.
I want to be elsewhere, elsewhere.
This is a poem about a horse that got tired.
Poor. Old. Tired. Horse.
I want to go home.
I want you to go home.
This is a poem which tells the story,
which is the story.
I don't know. I get lost.
If only they would stand still and let me.
Are you happy, sad, not happy, please come.
This is a poem for everyone.

The Three Ladies

I dreamt. I saw three ladies in a tree,
and the one that I saw most clearly
showed her favors unto me,
and I saw up her leg above the knee!

But when the time for love was come,
and of readiness I had made myself,
upon my head and shoulders
dropped the other two like an unquiet dew.

What were these two but the one?
I saw in their faces, I heard in their words,
wonder of wonders! it was the undoing of me
they came down to see!

Sister, they said to her who upon my lap
sat complacent, expectant:
he is dead in his head, and we
have errands, have errands . . .

Oh song of wistful night! Light shows
where it stops nobody knows, and two
are one, and three, to me, and to look
is not to read the book.

Oh one, two, three! Oh one, two three!
Three old ladies sat in a tree.

Oh No

If you wander far enough
you will come to it
and when you get there
they will give you a place to sit

for yourself only, in a nice chair,
and all your friends will be there
with smiles on their faces
and they will likewise all have places.

Goodbye

She stood at the window. There was
a sound, a light.
She stood at the window. A face.

Was it that she was looking for,
he thought. Was it that
she was looking for. He said,

turn from it, turn
from it. The pain is
not unpainful. Turn from it.

The act of her anger, of
the anger she felt then,
not turning to him.

The Interview

Light eyes would have been more fortunate.
They have cares like store windows.
All the water was shut off,
and winter settled in the house.

The first week they wrote a letter.
He wrote it.
She thought about it.
Peace was in the house like a broken staircase.

I was neat about it, she later wrote
to a relative in Spokane.
She spoke in accents low
as she told me.

A Wicker Basket

Comes the time when it's later
and onto your table the headwaiter
puts the bill, and very soon after
rings out the sound of lively laughter—

Picking up change, hands like a walrus,
and a face like a barndoor's,
and a head without any apparent size,
nothing but two eyes—

So that's you, man,
or me. I make it as I can,
I pick up, I go
faster than they know—

Out the door, the street like a night,
any night, and no one in sight,
but then, well, there she is,
old friend Liz—

And she opens the door of her cadillac,
I step in back,
and we're gone.
She turns me on—

There are very huge stars, man, in the sky,
and from somewhere very far off someone hands me a slice of
    ◁ apple pie,
with a gob of white, white ice cream on top of it,
and I eat it—

Slowly. And while certainly
they are laughing at me, and all around me is racket
of these cats not making it, I make it

in my wicker basket.

The Bed

She walks in beauty like a lake
and eats her steak
with fork and knife
and proves a proper wife.

Her room and board
he can afford, he has made friends
of common pains
and meets his ends.

Oh god, decry
such common finery as puts the need
before the bed, makes true what is
the lie indeed.

Just Friends

Out of the table endlessly rocking,
sea-shells, and firm,
I saw a face appear
which called me dear.

To be loved is half the battle
I thought.
To be
is to be better than is not.

Now when you are old what will you say?
You don't say,
she said.
That was on a Thursday.

Friday night I left
and haven't been back since.
Everything is water
if you look long enough.

The Wind

Whatever is to become of me
becomes daily as the acquaintance
with facts is made less the point,
and firm feelings are reencountered.

This morning I drank coffee and orange juice,
waiting for the biscuits which never came.
It is my own failing
because I cannot make them.

Praise god in women.
Give thanks to love in homes.
Without them all men
would starve to the bone.

Mother was helpful but essentially mistaken.
It is the second half of the 20th century.
I screamed that endlessly,
hearing it back distorted.

Who comes?
The light footsteps
down the hall
betoken

—in all her loveliness,
in all her grimness,
in all her asking and staying silent,
all mothers or potentials thereof.

There is no hymn yet written
that could
provoke beyond the laughter I feel
an occasion for this song—

But as love is long-winded,
the moving wind
describes its moving colors
of sound and flight.

Air: "Cat Bird Singing"

Cat bird singing
makes music like sounds coming

at night. The trees, goddamn them,
are huge eyes. They

watch, certainly, what
else should they do? My love

is a person of rare refinement,
and when she speaks,

there is another air,
melody—what Campion spoke of

with his
follow thy fair sunne unhappie shadow . . .

Catbird, catbird.
O lady hear me. I have no

other
voice left.

The Hero

Each voice which was asked
spoke its words, and heard
more than that, the fair question,
the onerous burden of the asking.

And so the hero, the
hero! stepped that gracefully
into his redemption, losing
or gaining life thereby.

Now we, now I
ask also, and burdened,
tied down, return
and seek the forest also.

Go forth, go forth,
saith the grandmother, the fire
of that old form, and turns
away from the form.

And the forest is dark,
mist hides it, trees
are dim, but I turn
to my father in the dark.

A spark, that spark of hope
which was burned out long ago,
the tedious echo
of the father image

—which only women bear,
also wear, old men, old cares,
and turn, and again find
the disorder in the mind.

Night is dark like the mind,
my mind is dark like the night.
O light the light! Old
foibles of the right.

Into that pit, now pit of
anywhere, the tears upon your hands,
how can you stand
it, I also turn.

I wear the face, I face
the right, the night, the way,
I go along the path
into the last and only dark,

hearing *hero! hero!*
a voice faint enough, a spark,
a glimmer grown dimmer through years
of old, old fears.

The Way

My love's manners in bed
are not to be discussed by me,
as mine by her
I would not credit comment upon gracefully.

Yet I ride by the margin of that lake in
the wood, the castle,
and the excitement of strongholds,
and have a small boy's notion of doing good.

Oh well, I will say here,
knowing each man,
let you find a good wife too,
and love her as hard as you can.

The Traveller

Into the forest again
whence all roads depend
this way and that
to lead him back.

Upon his shoulders
he places boulders,
upon his eye
the high wide sky.

A Marriage

The first retainer
he gave to her
was a golden
wedding ring.

The second—late at night
he woke up,
leaned over on an elbow,
and kissed her.

The third and the last—
he died with
and gave up loving
and lived with her.

She Went to Stay

Trying to chop mother down is like
hunting deer inside Russia
with phalangists for hat-pins.
I couldn't.

A Folk Song

for Phil

Hitch up honey for the
market race all
the way to the plaza!

If she don't run you
can push her like
hell. I know.

Ballad of the Despairing Husband

My wife and I lived all alone,
contention was our only bone.
I fought with her, she fought with me,
and things went on right merrily.

But now I live here by myself
with hardly a damn thing on the shelf,
and pass my days with little cheer
since I have parted from my dear.

Oh come home soon, I write to her.
Go fuck yourself, is her answer.
Now what is that, for Christian word?
I hope she feeds on dried goose turd.

But still I love her, yes I do.
I love her and the children too.
I only think it fit that she
should quickly come right back to me.

Ah no, she says, and she is tough,
and smacks me down with her rebuff.
Ah no, she says, I will not come
after the bloody things you've done.

Oh wife, oh wife—I tell you true,
I never loved no one but you.
I never will, it cannot be
another woman is for me.

That may be right, she will say then,
but as for me, there's other men.
And I will tell you I propose
to catch them firmly by the nose.

And I will wear what dresses I choose!
And I will dance, and what's to lose!
I'm free of you, you little prick,
and I'm the one can make it stick.

Was this the darling I did love?
Was this that mercy from above
did open violets in the spring—
and made my own worn self to sing?

She was. I know. And she is still,
and if I love her? then so I will.
And I will tell her, and tell her right . . .

Oh lovely lady, morning or evening or afternoon.
Oh lovely lady, eating with or without a spoon.
Oh most lovely lady, whether dressed or undressed or partly.
Oh most lovely lady, getting up or going to bed or sitting only.

Oh loveliest of ladies, than whom none is more fair, more
  ◁ gracious, more beautiful.
Oh loveliest of ladies, whether you are just or unjust, merciful,
  ◁ indifferent, or cruel.
Oh most loveliest of ladies, doing whatever, seeing whatever,
  ◁ being whatever.
Oh most loveliest of ladies, in rain, in shine, in any weather.

Oh lady, grant me time,
please, to finish my rhyme.

Damon & Pythias

When he got into bed,
he was dead.

Oh god, god, god, he said.
She watched him take off his shoes

and kneel there
to look for the change which had fallen

out of his pocket.
Old Mr. Jones

whom nobody loves
went to market for it,

and almost found it
under a table,

but by that time was unable.
And the other day two men,

who had been known as friends,
were said to be living together again.

If You

If you were going to get a pet
what kind of animal would you get.

A soft bodied dog, a hen—
feathers and fur to begin it again.

When the sun goes down and it gets dark
I saw an animal in a park.

Bring it home, to give it to you.
I have seen animals break in two.

You were hoping for something soft
and loyal and clean and wondrously careful—

a form of otherwise vicious habit
can have long ears and be called a rabbit.

Dead. Died. Will die. Want.
Morning, midnight. I asked you

if you were going to get a pet
what kind of animal would you get.

The Tunnel

Tonight, nothing is long enough—
time isn't.
Were there a fire,
it would burn now.

Were there a heaven,
I would have gone long ago.
I think that light
is the final image.

But time reoccurs,
love—and an echo.
A time passes
love in the dark.

The Saints

Heaven won't have to do with its multitudes.
There isn't room enough.
A thought we've all had perhaps,
now taken beyond that consideration.

Last night I saw several people
in a dream, in shapes
of all of this: faces and hands,
and things to say, too.

I love you, one said.
And I love you too. Let's
get out of this.
One said: I have to take a piss.

The door to the pantry was dark,
where the two crouched,
his hand on her back, her hand
on his back. I looked

at an evil, in the face.
I saw its place, in the universe,
and laughed back
until my mind cracked.

The Names

When they came near,
the one, two, three, four,
all five of us sat
in the broken seat.

Oh glad to see,
oh glad to be,
where company
is so derived
from sticks and stones,
bottles and bones.

A Gift of Great Value

Oh that horse I see so high
when the world shrinks into its
relationships, my mother
sees as well as I.

She was born, but I bore with her.
This horse was a mighty occasion!
The intensity of its feet! The height
of its immense body!

Now then in wonder at evening, at
the last small entrance of the night,
my mother calls it, and I
call it *my father*.

With angry face, with no
rights, with impetuosity and
sterile vision—and a great
wind we ride.

My Love

It falleth like a stick.
    It lieth like air.
It is wonderment and bewilderment,
    to test true.

It is no thing, but of two,
    equal: as the mind turns to it,
it doubleth,
    as one alone.

Where it is, there is
    everywhere, separate,
yet few—as dew
    to night is.

Saturday Afternoon

It is like a monster come to dinner,
and the dinner table is set,
the fire in the fireplace,
good luck to good humor—

The monster you love is home again,
and he tells you the stories of the world,
big cities, small men
and women.

Make room for the furry, wooden eyed
monster. He is my friend
whom you burn.
Amen.

The Invoice

I once wrote a letter as follows:
dear Jim, I would like to borrow
200 dollars from you
to see me through.

I also wrote another: dearest M/
please come.
There is no one
here at all.

I got word today,
viz: hey
sport, how are you making it?
And, why don't you get with it.

Somewhere

The galloping collection of boards
are the house which I afforded
one evening to walk into
just as the night came down.

Dark inside, the candle
lit of its own free will, the attic
groaned then, the stairs
led me up into the air.

From outside, it must have seemed
a wonder that it was
the inside *he* as *me* saw
in the dark there.

New Year's

The end of the year wears its face in the moon against the
◁ disguises one would otherwise put upon it.
It is the mild temper of midnight that embarrasses us and oh!
◁ we turn away into reassuring daylight but backwards.

If it were the forward motion one wanted—
What tempers would not be resolved, can one keep the night
◁ out of it as or when it was there?

Darling (she had gone) we speak as if there never were an
◁ answer.
We speak (to the back, to sleep, to heads). We are alone in the
◁ new minute, hour, or year, or nowhere.

House. Your hand is too far from me. Tree, speak. The
◁ moon is white in the branches, the night is white in the
◁ mind of it.
Love, tell me the time. What time is it? The second, the
◁ moment moving in the moon?

Of the strangeness of bending backwards until the mind is an
◁ instant of mind in the moon's light white upon an
Endless black desert, the sand, in the night of the last
◁ moment of the year.

Song

God give you pardon from gratitude
and other mild forms of servitude—

and make peace for all of us
with what is easy.

Lady Bird

A lady asks me
and I would tell

what is it
she has found the burden of.

To be happy
now she cries, and all things

turn backward
and impossible.

God knows that I love her,
and would comfort her—

but the invention is
a parallel sufferance.

Mine for hers,
hers for mine.

For a Friend

Who remembers him also, he thinks
(but to himself and as himself).

Himself alone is dominant
in a world of no one else.

Entre Nous

If I can't hope then to hell with it.
I don't want to live like this?

Like this, he said. Where were you?
She was around in back of the bureau

where he pushed her?
Hell no, she just fell.

Sing Song

I sing the song of the sleeping wife,
who married to sleep,
who would not sleep simply to get married;

who can be up at dawn, yet
never cannot go to sleep if there is
good reason not to go to sleep;

who sleeps to sleep,
who has no other purpose in mind,
who wouldn't even hear you if you asked her.

And

A pretty party for people
to become engaged in, she was

twentythree, he
was a hundred and twentyseven times

all the times, over and over
and under and under she went

down stairs, through doorways,
glass, alabaster, an iron shovel

stood waiting and
she lifted it to dig

back
and back to mother,

father and brother,
grandfather and grandmother—

They are all dead now.

Heroes

In all those stories the hero
is beyond himself into the next
thing, be it those labors
of Hercules, or Aeneas going into death.

I thought the instant of the one humanness
in Virgil's plan of it
was that it was of course human enough to die,
yet to come back, as he said, *hoc opus, hic labor est*.

That was the Cumaean Sibyl speaking.
This is Robert Creeley, and Virgil
is dead now two thousand years, yet Hercules
and the *Aeneid*, yet all that industrious wis-

dom lives in the way the mountains
and the desert are waiting
for the heroes, and death also
can still propose the old labors.

Going to Bed

That dim shattering character of nerves
which creates faces in the dark
speaks of the heaven and hell
as a form of corporate existence.

Oh don't say it isn't so,
think to understand if
the last time you looked
you were still a man.

It is a viscous form of self-
propulsion that lets the feet grip
the floor, as the head
lifts to the door,

lurches, ghostwise, out, and to
the window to fall through,
yet closes it to let
the cat out too.

After that, silence, silence.
On the floor the hands
find quiet, the mouth goes lax.
Oh! Look forward to get back.

Oh wisdom to find fault with
what is after all a plan.

The Flower

I think I grow tensions
like flowers
in a wood where
nobody goes.

Each wound is perfect,
encloses itself in a tiny
imperceptible blossom,
making pain.

Pain is a flower like that one,
like this one,
like that one,
like this one.

The Letter

I did not expect you
to stay married to
one man all your life,
no matter you were his wife.

I thought the pain was endless—
but the form existent,
as it is form,
and as such I loved it.

I loved you as well
even as you might tell,
giving evidence
as to how much was penitence.

The Place

What is the form is the gro-
tesquerie—the accident
of the moon's light
on your face.

Oh love, an empty table!
An empty bottle also.
But no trick will go
so far but not further.

The end of the year is a division, a drunken derision
of composition's accident.
We both fell.

I fell. You fell.
In hell we will tell of it.
Form's accidents, we move back-
wards to love . . .

The movement of the
sentence tells me of you
as it was the bottle we drank?
No. It was no accident.

Agh, form is what happens?
Form is an accompaniment.
I to love, you to love:
syntactic accident.

It will all come true,
in a year.
The empty bottle, the empty table,
tell where we were.

The Souvenir

Passing into the wilderness of twisted trees,
below the goats and sheep look up at us,
as we climb the hill for our picnic
years ago.

For the New Year

From something in the trees
looking down at me

or else an inexact sign
of a remote and artificial tenderness—

a woman who passes me
and who will not consider me—

things I have tried to take
with which to make something

like a toy for my children
and a story to be quietly forgotten.

Oh God, send me an omen
that I may remember more often.

Keep me, see to me,
let me look.

Being unsure, there is the fate
of doing nothing right.

The Door

for Robert Duncan

It is hard going to the door
cut so small in the wall where
the vision which echoes loneliness
brings a scent of wild flowers in a wood.

What I understood, I understand.
My mind is sometime torment,
sometimes good and filled with livelihood,
and feels the ground.

But I see the door,
and knew the wall, and wanted the wood,
and would get there if I could
with my feet and hands and mind.

Lady, do not banish me
for digressions. My nature
is a quagmire of unresolved
confessions. Lady, I follow.

I walked away from myself,
I left the room, I found the garden,
I knew the woman
in it, together we lay down.

Dead night remembers. In December
we change, not multiplied but dispersed,
sneaked out of childhood,
the ritual of dismemberment.

Mighty magic is a mother,
in her there is another issue
of fixture, repeated form, the race renewal,
the charge of the command.

The garden echoes across the room.
It is fixed in the wall like a mirror
that faces a window behind you
and reflects the shadows.

May I go now?
Am I allowed to bow myself down
in the ridiculous posture of renewal,
of the insistence of which I am the virtue?

Nothing for You is untoward.
Inside You would also be tall,
more tall, more beautiful.
Come toward me from the wall, I want to be with You.

So I screamed to You,
who hears as the wind, and changes
multiply, invariably,
changes in the mind.

Running to the door, I ran down
as a clock runs down. Walked backwards,
stumbled, sat down
hard on the floor near the wall.

Where were You.
How absurd, how vicious.
There is nothing to do but get up.
My knees were iron, I rusted in worship, of You.

For that one sings, one
writes the spring poem, one goes on walking.
The Lady has always moved to the next town
and you stumble on after Her.

The door in the wall leads to the garden
where in the sunlight sit
the Graces in long Victorian dresses,
of which my grandmother had spoken.

History sings in their faces.
They are young, they are obtainable,
and you follow after them also
in the service of God and Truth.

But the Lady is indefinable,
she will be the door in the wall
to the garden in sunlight.
I will go on talking forever.

I will never get there.
Oh Lady, remember me
who in Your service grows older
not wiser, no more than before.

How can I die alone.
Where will I be then who am now alone,
what groans so pathetically
in this room where I am alone?

I will go to the garden.
I will be a romantic. I will sell
myself in hell,
in heaven also I will be.

In my mind I see the door,
I see the sunlight before me across the floor
beckon to me, as the Lady's skirt
moves small beyond it.

The Hill

It is some time since I have been
to what it was had once turned me backwards,
and made my head into
a cruel instrument.

It is simple
to confess. Then done,
to walk away, walk away,
to come again.

But that form, I must answer,
is dead in me, completely,
and I will not allow it
to reappear—

Saith perversity, the willful,
the magnanimous cruelty,
which is in me
like a hill.

3

1959 • 1960

The Awakening

for Charles Olson

He feels small as he awakens,
but in the stream's sudden mirror,
a pool of darkening water,
sees his size with his own two eyes.

The trees are taller here,
fall off to no field or clearing,
and depend on the inswept air
for the place in which he finds himself thus lost.

I was going on to tell you
when the door bell rang it was
another story as I know
previously had happened, had occurred.

That was a woman's impression
of the wonders of the morning, the same place,
whiter air now, and strong breezes
move the birds off in that first freshening.

O wisest of gods! Unnatural prerogatives
would err to concur, would fall deafened
between the seen, the green green,
and the ring of a far off telephone.

God is no bone of whitened contention.
God is not air, nor hair, is not
a conclusive concluding
to remote yearnings. He moves

only as I move, you also move to
the awakening, across long rows, of beds,
stumble breathlessly, on leg pins and crutch,
moving at all as all men, because you must.

Kore

As I was walking
   I came upon
chance walking
   the same road upon.

As I sat down
   by chance to move
later
   if and as I might,

light the wood was,
   light and green,
and what I saw
   before I had not seen.

It was a lady
   accompanied
by goat men
   leading her.

Her hair held earth.
   Her eyes were dark.
A double flute
   made her move.

"O love,
   where are you
leading
   me now?"

The Rain

All night the sound had
come back again,
and again falls
this quiet, persistent rain.

What am I to myself
that must be remembered,
insisted upon
so often? Is it

that never the ease,
even the hardness,
of rain falling
will have for me

something other than this,
something not so insistent—
am I to be locked in this
final uneasiness.

Love, if you love me,
lie next to me.
Be for me, like rain,
the getting out

of the tiredness, the fatuousness, the semi-
lust of intentional indifference.
Be wet
with a decent happiness.

The Woman

I called her across the room,
could see that what she stood on
held her up, and now she came
as if she moved in time.

In time to what she moved,
her hands, her hair, her eyes, all things
by which I took her to be there
did come along.

It was not right or wrong
but signally despair, to be about
to speak to her
as if her substance shouted.

Midnight

When the rain stops
and the cat drops
out of the tree
to walk

away, when the rain stops,
when the others come home, when
the phone stops,
the drip of water, the

potential of a caller
any Sunday afternoon.

The Kid

If it falls flat
I'm used to it. Yet
cannot grow when
I can't begin again.

Nowise to secure
what's left to others. They
forget.
But I remember.

How carelessly ease falls
around me! All the trees
have it, the leaves
all green!

I want to grow in ground too,
want it to come true
what they said about if you planted
the acorn the tree would grow.

Lady in Black

The mental picture which the
lady in black if she be
coming, or going,
offered by the occasion

to the church, behind the
black car, lately
stepped out of, and
her dress

falls, lets
all eyes as if
people were
looking

see
her still
an attitude
perplexing.

The Plan

Daytime
wonder at
the quieter possibilities
of slumber,

deep sleep,
in peace
some place the mind
will yet escape.

Or else, truth,
the mind
this time at last
trapped:

no voice, no
way left. The
hand at last
can tighten.

Why live
in the middle
of this
damned muddle?

Why not—
lesser thing?
find out
what another will bring.

Woman, addressed,
speaks easily
unless
she is depressed.

Children, wiser,
make their own
things unless
thrown under

the way, the way
it was yesterday, will
be also today
and tomorrow.

The Joke

There was a joke
went on a walk like
over the hill, and there before them
these weary travellers
saw valleys and farms
of muscles, tits raised high
in the sky of their vision which bewildered
them. They were
no ordinary men but those who come
innocent, late and alone
to women and a home, and keep on talking
and keep on walking.

The Song

It still makes sense
to know the song after all.

My wiseness I wear
in despair of something better.

I am all beggar,
I am all ears.

Soon everything will be sold
and I can go back home

by myself again
and try to be a man.

The Bird

What did you say to me
    that I had not heard.
She said she saw
    a small bird.

Where was it.
    In a tree.
Ah, he said, I thought
    you spoke to me.

Yellow

He wants to be an Indian,
someone else a white man,
or black man, pacing
this to a reason simply given.

What do they put in the graves of
dissatisfied men?
What for the women
who denied them, changing

their colors into
greens, reds, blues,
yellow. Her hands were
yellow, her eyes were

yellow. The Indians want
her to be their queen
because she is such a
lovely color.

The Cracks

Don't step
so lightly. Break
your back, missed
the step. Don't go

away mad, lady in
the nightmare. You
are central,
even necessary.

I will attempt to describe you.
I will be completely without
face, a lost
chance, nothing at all left.

"Well," he said
as he was leaving,
"blood
tells."

But you remembered quickly
other times, other faces,
and I slipped between the good
intentions, breathlessly.

What a good boy am I who
wants to. Will you,
mother, come quickly,
won't you. Why not

go quietly, be left
with a memory
or an insinuation or two
of cracks in a pavement.

Jack's Blues

I'm going to roll up
a monkey and smoke it, put
an elephant in the pot. I'm going out
and never come back.

What's better than that.
Lying on your back, flat
on your back with your
eyes to the view.

Oh the view is blue, I saw that
too, yesterday and you,
red eyes and blue,
funked.

I'm going to roll up
a rug and smoke it, put
the car in the garage and I'm
gone, like a sad old candle.

Out of Sight

He thinks
always things
will be simpler,
with face

of a clown
so that the mouth
rolls down, then
the eye shuts

as a fist
to hold patience,
patience,
in the locked mind.

A Token

My lady
fair with
soft
arms, what

can I say to
you—words, words
as if all
worlds were there.

The Man

He hie fie finger
speak in simple sound
feels much better
lying down.

He toes is broken
all he foot go
rotten
now. He look

he hurt bad, see
danger all around he
no see before
come down on him.

The Memory

Like a river she was,
huge roily mass of water
carrying tree trunks
and divers drunks.

Like a Priscilla, a feminine Benjamin,
a whore gone right over
the falls,
she was.

Did you know her.
Did you love her, brother.
Did wonder pour down
on the whole goddamn town.

To And

To and
back and forth,
direction
is a third

or simple fourth
of the intention
like it
goes and goes.

No
more snow this
winter?
No more snow.

Then what replaces
all the faces,
wasted,
wasted.

A Wish

So much rain
to make the mud again,
trees green
and flowers also.

The water which
ran up the sun
and down again,
it is the same.

A man of supple
yielding manner
might, too, discover
ways of water.

Song

What I took in my hand
grew in weight. You must
understand it
was not obscene.

Night comes. We sleep.
Then if you know what
say it.
Don't pretend.

Guises are
what enemies wear. You
and I live
in a prayer.

Helpless. Helpless,
should I speak.
Would you.
What do you think of me.

No woman ever was,
was wiser
than you. None is
more true.

But fate, love, fate
scares me. What
I took in my hand
grows in weight.

The Sign Board

The quieter the people are
the slower the time passes

until there is a solitary man
sitting in the figure of silence.

Then scream at him,
come here you idiot it's going to go off.

A face that is no face
but the features, of a face, pasted

on a face until that face
is faceless, answers by

a being nothing there
where there was a man.

Not Now

I can see you,
hairy, extended, vulnerable,
but how did you get up there.
Where were you going all alone,

why didn't you wait
for the others to come home
to go too, they would
have gone with you.

The Time

They walk in and fall into
the large crack in the floor
with the room upended on side
to make the floor a wall.

Upwards or downwards now
they fall into the crack,
having no floor
or ceiling to refer to,

what time comes to,
the place it all goes into.
All that was an instant ago
is gone now.

Song

Those rivers run from that land
to sea. The wind
finds trees to move,
then goes again.

And me, why me
on any day might be
favored with kind prosperity
or sunk in wretched misery.

I cannot stop the weather
by putting together
myself and another
to stop those rivers.

Or hold the wind
with my hand from the tree,
the mind from the thing,
love from her or me.

Be natural, while alive.
Dead, we die to that
also, and go another
course, I hope.

And me, why me
on any day might be
favored with kind prosperity
or sunk in wretched misery.

You I want back of me
in the life we have here,
waiting to see
what becomes of it.

Call, call loud,
I will hear you, or if
not me, the wind will
for the sake of the tree.

The Rescue

The man sits in a timelessness
with the horse under him in time
to a movement of legs and hooves
upon a timeless sand.

Distance comes in from the foreground
present in the picture as time
he reads outward from
and comes from that beginning.

A wind blows in
and out and all about the man
as the horse ran
and runs to come in time.

A house is burning in the sand.
A man and horse are burning.
The wind is burning.
They are running to arrive.

The Paradox

Looking down at her
long hair,
we saw the position
in which we placed her.

Yet our own
a formula, the street
she walked up
she looked down on.

The End of the Day

Oh who is
so cosy with
despair and
all, they will

not come,
rejuvenated, to
the last spectacle
of the day. Look!

the sun is
sinking, now
it's
gone. Night,

good and sweet
night, good
night, good, good
night, has come.

The Women

"What he holds to
         is a cross
and by just that much
         is his load increased."

•

"Yet the eyes
         cannot die in a face
whereof the hands
         are nailed in place."

•

"I wish I might grow
         tall like a tree
to be cut down
         to bear such beauty."

For Fear

For fear I want
to make myself again
under the thumb
of old love, old time

subservience
and pain, bent
into a nail that will
not come out.

Why, love, does it
make such a difference
not to be heard
in spite of self

or what we may feel,
one for the other,
but as a hammer
to drive again

bent nail
into old hurt?

The Gift

He hands
down the gift
as from a great
height, his

precious
understanding clothed
in miraculous
fortitude. This

is the present
of the ages, all
rewards
in itself.

But the lady—
she, disdain-
ful, all
in white for

this occasion—cries
out petulantly, is
that all, is
that all.

The House

for Louis Zukofsky

Mud put
upon mud,
lifted
to make room,

house
a cave,
and
colder night.

To sleep
in, live in,
to come in
from heat,

all form derived
from kind,
built
with that in mind.

Young Woman

Young woman, older
woman, as soon as the
words begin, you
leave, rightly.

How pace yourself behind,
how follow when it is you
also who leads, to be
followed, and why not.

Is there a patience
we learn, barely, hardly,
a condition into which we
are suspended?

Is there a place for us,
do you know it well
enough that without thought
it can be found?

I think, and
therefore I am not,
who was to have been, as you,
something else.

The Pool

My embarrassment at his nakedness,
at the pool's edge,
and my wife, with his,
standing, watching—

this was a freedom
not given me who am
more naked,
less contained

by my own white flesh
and the ability
to take quietly
what comes to me.

The sense of myself
separate, grew
a white mirror
in the quiet water

he breaks with his hands
and feet, kicking,
pulls up to land
on the edge by the feet

of these women
who must know
that for each
man is a speech

describes him, makes
the day grow white
and sure, a quietness of water
in the mind,

lets hang, descriptive
as a risk, something
for which he cannot find
a means or time.

Air: "The Love of a Woman"

The love of a woman
is the possibility which
surrounds her as hair
her head, as the love of her

follows and describes
her. But what if
they die, then there is
still the aura

left, left sadly, but
hovers in the air, surely,
where this had taken place?
Then sing, of her, of whom

it will be said, he
sang of her, it was the
song he made which made her
happy, so she lived.

Mind's Heart

Mind's heart, it must
be that some
truth lies locked
in you.

Or else, lies, all
lies, and no man
true enough to know
the difference.

The Name

Be natural,
wise
as you can be,
my daughter,

let my name
be in you flesh
I gave you
in the act of

loving your mother,
all your days
her ways,
the woman in you

brought from
sensuality's measure,
no other,
there was no thought

of it but such
pleasure all women
must be in her,
as you. But not wiser,

not more of nature
than her hair,
the eyes
she gives you.

There will not be another
woman such as you
are. Remember
your mother,

the way you came,
the days of waiting.
Be natural,
daughter, wise

as you can be,
all my daughters,
be women
for men

when that time comes.
Let the rhetoric
stay with me
your father. Let

me talk about it,
saving you such
vicious self-
exposure, let you

pass it on
in you. I cannot
be more than the man
who watches.

The First Time

We are given a chance,
among the worst something left
otherwise, hopeful
circumstance.

As I spoke to you,
once,
I loved you
as simply as that.

Now to go back,
I cannot
but going on,
will not forget the first time.

You likewise
with me must be
testament
to pain's indifference.

We are only careful
for such a memory, more
careful, I think,
than we ever thought to be.

The Figures

The stillness
of the wood,
the figures formed

by hands so still
they touched it
to be one

hand holding one
hand, faces
without eyes,

bodies of wooden
stone, so still
they will not move

from that quiet
action ever
again. Did the man

who made them find
a like quiet? In
the act of making them

it must have been
so still he heard the wood
and felt it with his hands

moving into
the forms
he has given to them,

one by singular
one, so quiet,
so still.

The Rose

for Bobbie

Up and down
she walks, listless
form, a movement
quietly misled.

Now, speak to her.
"Did you want
to go, then why
don't you."

She went. There were
things she left
in the room
as a form of it.

He follows, walking.
Where do they walk now?
Do they talk now
where they are

in that other place
grown monstrous,
quiet quiet air
as breath.

And all about a rosy
mark discloses
her nature
to him, vague and unsure.

There roses, here roses,
flowers, a pose of
nature, her
nature has disclosed to him.

Yet breathing, crouched
in the dark,
he is there
also, recovers,

to bring her back
to herself, himself.
The room wavers,
wavers.

And as if,
as if a cloud had
broken at last
open

and all the rain
from that,
from that had fallen
on them,

on them there is a mark
of her nature, her flowers,
and his room, his nature,
to come home to.

The Eye

Moon
and clouds, will
we drift

higher
than that we
look at,

moon's and
mind's
eye.

Love Comes Quietly

Love comes quietly,
finally, drops
about me, on me,
in the old ways.

What did I know
thinking myself
able to go
alone all the way.

After Mallarmé

Stone,
like stillness,
around you my
mind sits, it is

a proper form
for
it, like
stone, like

compression itself,
fixed fast,
grey,
without a sound.

The People

Wistful,
they speak of
satis-
faction, love

and divers
other
things. It
comforts,

it surprises
them, the
old
remembrances,

like hands to
hold them
safe and
warm. So

must it be, then,
some god looks
truly down
upon them.

The Wife

I know two women
    and the one
is tangible substance,
    flesh and bone.

The other in my mind
    occurs.
She keeps her strict
    proportion there.

But how should I
    propose to live
with two such creatures
    in my bed—

or how shall he
    who has a wife
yield two to one
    and watch the other die.

The Snow

The broken snow should leave the traces
of yesterday's walks, the paths worn in,
and bring friends to our door
somewhere in the dark winter.

Sometime in April I will get at last
the flowers promised you long ago,—
to think of it
will help us through.

The night is a pleasure to us,
I think sleeping, and what warmth secures
me you bring,
giving at last freely of yourself.

Myself was old, was confused, was wanting,—
to sing of an old song,
through the last echo of hurting,
brought now home.

Fire

Clear smoke,
a fire in the far off
haze of summer,
burning somewhere.

What is
a lonely heart for
if not
for itself alone.

Do the questions
answer themselves,
all wonder
brought to a reckoning?

When you are done,
I am done,
then it seems that
one by one

we can leave it all,
to go on.

For Friendship

For friendship
make a chain that holds,
to be bound to
others, two by two,

a walk, a garland,
handed by hands
that cannot move
unless they hold.

The Gesture

The gesture she makes
to rise,
all her flesh is white,
and tired.

Now morning, now
night, and sun
shines as
moonlight.

Sun, for her
make do
light with bright
moon and

love and children
sleeping,
in her tired
mind's keeping.

For Love

for Bobbie

Yesterday I wanted to
speak of it, that sense above
the others to me
important because all

that I know derives
from what it teaches me.
Today, what is it that
is finally so helpless,

different, despairs of its own
statement, wants to
turn away, endlessly
to turn away.

If the moon did not . . .
no, if you did not
I wouldn't either, but
what would I not

do, what prevention, what
thing so quickly stopped.
That is love yesterday
or tomorrow, not

now. Can I eat
what you give me. I
have not earned it. Must
I think of everything

as earned. Now love also
becomes a reward so
remote from me I have
only made it with my mind.

Here is tedium,
despair, a painful

sense of isolation and
whimsical if pompous

self-regard. But that image
is only of the mind's
vague structure, vague to me
because it is my own.

Love, what do I think
to say. I cannot say it.
What have you become to ask,
what have I made you into,

companion, good company,
crossed legs with skirt, or
soft body under
the bones of the bed.

Nothing says anything
but that which it wishes
would come true, fears
what else might happen in

some other place, some
other time not this one.
A voice in my place, an
echo of that only in yours.

Let me stumble into
not the confession but
the obsession I begin with
now. For you

also (also)
some time beyond place, or
place beyond time, no
mind left to

say anything at all,
that face gone, now.
Into the company of love
it all returns.

Words

There is, in short,
a counter stress,
     born of the sexual shock,
          which survives it
consonant with the moon,
     to keep its own mind.

WILLIAM CARLOS WILLIAMS
To Daphne and Virginia

Things continue, but my sense is that I have, at best, simply taken place with that fact. I see no progress in time or any other such situation. So it is that what I feel, in the world, is the one thing I know myself to be, for that instant. I will never know myself otherwise.

Intentions are the variability of all these feelings, moments of that possibility. How can I ever assume that they must come to this or that substance? I am trying to say that what I think to say is of no help to me—and yet insist on my seriousness, which is a sense of my nature I would like to admire.

Words will not say anything more than they do, and my various purposes will not understand them more than what they say.

1967

I

The Rhythm

It is all a rhythm,
from the shutting
door, to the window
opening,

the seasons, the sun's
light, the moon,
the oceans, the
growing of things,

the mind in men
personal, recurring
in them again,
thinking the end

is not the end, the
time returning,
themselves dead but
someone else coming.

If in death I am dead,
then in life also
dying, dying . . .
And the women cry and die.

The little children
grow only to old men.
The grass dries,
the force goes.

But is met by another
returning, oh not mine,
not mine, and
in turn dies.

The rhythm which projects
from itself continuity
bending all to its force
from window to door,
from ceiling to floor,
light at the opening,
dark at the closing.

The Rocks

Trying to think of
some way out, the
rocks of thought

which displace,
dropped in
the water,

much else.
So life is
water, love also

has substance of
like kind.
Wanting

water a Sunday
morning God will
not provide—

is it my
wife, her warmth
lying

beside me, is
that sense of warm
moistness the condition

in which all grows?
Drop
the rock,

think well, think
well of me.

Water

The sun's
sky in
form of
blue sky
that

water will
never make
even
in
reflection.

Sing, song,
mind's form
feeling
if
mistaken,

shaken,
broken water's
forms, love's
error
in water.

The Mountains
in the Desert

The mountains blue now
at the back of my head,
such geography of self and soul
brought to such limit of sight,

I cannot relieve it
nor leave it, my mind locked
in seeing it
as the light fades.

Tonight let me go
at last out of whatever
mind I thought to have,
and all the habits of it.

Waiting

He pushes behind the words
which, awkward, catch
and turn him to a disturbed
and fumbling man.

What if it all stops.
Then silence
is as silence was
again.

What if the last time
he was moved to touch,
work out in his own mind,
such limits was the last—

and then a quiet, a dull
space of hanging actions, all
depending on some time
has come and gone.

God help him then
if such things can.
That risk
is all there is.

The Invitation

If it ever is
as it will be,
then enough is
enough. They

think in clusters
round the interminable
subject all but
lost to my mind.

Well, here I am,
they say, together.
Or here you are,
them, and it.

Let's build a house of
human pieces, arms
and hair, not telling
any one. Shout

from the feet, face
facts as accumulations,
we can
do it.

Or and, and as
it's done, what flesh
can do, home again
we'll say,

we'll fall down streets
rolling,
balls
of clear substance.

The Turn

Each way the turn
twists, to be apprehended:
now she is
there, now she

is not, goes, but
did she, having gone,
went before
the eye saw

nothing. The tree
cannot walk, all its
going must
be violence. They listen

to the saw cut, the
roots scream. And in eating
even a stalk of celery
there will be pathetic screaming.

But what we want
is not what we get.
What we saw, we think
we will see again?

We will not. Moving,
we will
move, and then
stop.

For W.C.W.

The rhyme is after
all the repeated
insistence.

There, you say, and
there, and there,
and *and* becomes

just so. And
what one wants is
what one wants,

yet complexly
as you
say.

Let's
let it go.
I want—

Then there is—
and,
I want.

Song

The grit
of things,
a measure
resistant—

times walk-
ing, talk-
ing, telling
lies and

all the other
places, no
one ever
quite the same.

The Fire

Oh flame falling, as shaken, as the stories
my daughter sees in the light, forming, seeing
the simple burning as an action which to speak of
now I complicate, with my own burning, her story.

Then it all goes, saying, here they were, and are,
and will be again, as I used to think, to remember,
then they were here, and now, again, they are.

What in the light's form finds her face,
makes of her eyes the simple grace.

For No Clear Reason

I dreamt last night
the fright was over, that
the dust came, and then water,
and women and men, together
again, and all was quiet
in the dim moon's light.

A paean of such patience—
laughing, laughing at me,
and the days extend over
the earth's great cover,
grass, trees, and flower-
ing season, for no clear reason.

The Messengers

for Allen Ginsberg

The huge dog, Broderick, and
the smile of the quick eyes
of Allen light a kind world.

Their feelings, under some distance
of remote skin, must touch,
wondering at what impatience does

block them. So little love
to share among so many, so much
yellow-orange hair, on the one,

and on the other, such a darkness
of long hanging hair now, such
slightness of body, and a voice that

rises on the sounds of feeling.
Aie! It raises the world, lifts,
falls, like a sudden sunlight, like

that edge of the black night sweeps
the low lying fields, of soft grasses,
bodies, fills them with quiet longing.

For Leslie

For you there ought
to be words as something
at least to say

of what couldn't be
then, the whole
sense crowded, almost

a comfortable agony
so full
I felt it.

Two years go,
the same wide sky
sits over us.

There, the grave is
I cannot
even go to

under some trees
in the grass
of someone's cemetery.

What argument can be
used now, the light so
strikes in,

so blonde you are,
so different from our darkness,
your eyes such blue.

I

"is the grandson
of Thomas L. Creeley, who acquired
eight acres of Belmont land around 1880 and

continued

"His house was numbered 375
Common st.

and his farm lands,
through the heart of which the present Creeley
rd. runs, adjoined

the Chenery holdings and extended
toward Waverly from upper
Common st.
                    The author's father, the late
Dr. Oscar Creeley,
was a prominent Watertown physician
for many years
                    and headed
the staff of Symmes Hospital in Arlington."

I, is late

But I saw a picture of him once, T.L.
in a chair in Belmont, or it was his invalid
and patient wife they told me sat there, he
was standing, long and steady faced,
a burden to him she was, and the son. The
other child had died

They waited, so my father
who also died when I is four gave all
to something like
the word "adjoined," "extended"
so I feels

I sees the time as long and wavering
grass in all about the lot in all that
cemetery again the old man owned a part of
so they couldn't dig him up.

Something

I approach with such
a careful tremor, always
I feel the finally foolish

question of how it is,
then, supposed to be felt,
and by whom. I remember

once in a rented room on
27th street, the woman I loved
then, literally, after we

had made love on the large
bed sitting across from
a basin with two faucets, she

had to pee but was nervous,
embarrassed I suppose I
would watch her who had but

a moment ago been completely
open to me, naked, on
the same bed. Squatting, her

head reflected in the mirror,
the hair dark there, the
full of her face, the shoulders,

sat spread-legged, turned on
one faucet and shyly pissed. What
love might learn from such a sight.

Walking

In my head I am
walking but I am not
in my head, where

is there to walk,
not thought of, is
the road itself more

than seen. I think
it might be, feel
as my feet do, and

continue, and
at last reach, slowly,
one end of my intention.

The Language

Locate *I*
love you some-
where in

teeth and
eyes, bite
it but

take care not
to hurt, you
want so

much so
little. Words
say everything.

I
love you
again,

then what
is emptiness
for. To

fill, fill.
I heard words
and words full

of holes
aching. Speech
is a mouth.

The Window

Position is where you
put it, where it is,
did you, for example, that

large tank there, silvered,
with the white church along-
side, lift

all that, to what
purpose? How
heavy the slow

world is with
everything put
in place. Some

man walks by, a
car beside him on
the dropped

road, a leaf of
yellow color is
going to

fall. It
all drops into
place. My

face is heavy
with the sight. I can
feel my eye breaking.

The Chance

For whatever, it could
be done, simply
remove it, cut the

offending member. Once
in a photograph by
Frederick Sommer a leg

lay on what was apparently
black velvet cut
from its attachment

to the rest, the foot
showing the incised
wound whereof

the beauty
of all
reasons.

Hello

With a quick
jump he caught
the edge of

her eye and
it tore, down,
ripping. She

shuddered,
with the unexpected
assault, but

to his vantage
he held by
what flesh was left.

Quick-Step

More gaily, dance
with such ladies make
a circumstance of dancing.

Let them lead
around and around, all
awkwardness apart.

There is
an easy grace gained
from falling forward

in time, in
simple time to
all their graces.

Variations

There is love only
as love is. These
senses recreate
their definition—a hand

holds within itself
all reason. The eyes
have seen such
beauty they close.

But continue. So the voice
again, *these senses recreate*
their singular condition
felt, and felt again.

I hear. I hear
the mind close, the voice
go on beyond it,
the hands open.

Hard, they hold so
closely themselves, only,
empty grasping of
such sensation.

Hear, there where
the echoes are
louder, clearer,
senses of sound

opening and closing,
no longer love's
only, mind's intention,
eyes' sight, hands holding—

broken to echoes, *these
senses recreate*
their definition. I hear
the mind close.

There Is

There is
as we go we
see there
is a hairy
hole there is
a darkness ex-
panded by
there is a
sense of some
imminence imman-
ence there is
a subject placed
by the verb a
conjunction coord-
inate lines
a graph of indeterminate
feelings there is
sorry for itself
lonely generally
unhappy in its
circumstances.

The Measure

I cannot
move backward
or forward.
I am caught

in the time
as measure.
What we think
of we think of—

of no other reason
we think than
just to think—
each for himself.

The Woman

I have never
clearly given to you
the associations
you have for me, you

with such
divided presence my dream
does not show
you. I do not dream.

I have compounded
these sensations, the
accumulation of the things
left me by you.

Always your
tits, not breasts, but
harsh sudden rises
of impatient flesh

on the chest—is it
mine—which flower
against the vagueness
of the air you move in.

You walk
such a shortness
of intent strides, your
height is so low,

in my hand
I feel the weight
of yours there,
one over one

or both, as you
pivot upon me, the
same weight grown
as the hair, the

second of your attributes,
falls to
cover us. We
couple but lie against

no surface, have
lifted as you again
grow small
against myself, into

the air. The
air the third of
the signs you
are known by: a

quiet, a
soughing silence,
the winds lightly
moved. Then

your
mouth, it
opens not
speaking, touches,

wet, on me. Then
I scream, I
sing such as is
given to me, roar-

ing unheard,
like stark sight
sees itself
inverted

into dark
turned. Onanistic,
I feel around
myself what

you have left me
with, wetness, pools
of it, my skin
drips.

The Pattern

As soon as
I speak, I
speaks. It

wants to
be free but
impassive lies

in the direction
of its
words. Let

x equal x, x
also
equals x. I

speak to
hear myself
speak? I

had not thought
that some-
thing had such

undone. It
was an idea
of mine.

The Mechanic

Were we now to fall
to our stubborn knees
and sink to rest, my-
self sunk in yours, then

what would hold us
together but uninteresting
weight. Do you believe
love, and how much.

Walls

Walls are
relief in lifting
themselves. Let

you also
lift yourself,
selves, shelves.

"I Keep to Myself
Such Measures . . ."

I keep to myself such
measures as I care for,
daily the rocks
accumulate position.

There is nothing
but what thinking makes
it less tangible. The mind,
fast as it goes, loses

pace, puts in place of it
like rocks simple markers,
for a way only to
hopefully come back to

where it cannot. All
forgets. My mind sinks.
I hold in both hands such weight
it is my only description.

The Dream

1

Such perfection
of dream would
first hurt, would

tear impression
from impression
making a fabric

of pain. Then
begin again
its own insistence.

In the dream
I see
two faces turned,

one of which
I assume mine, one
of which I assume.

It is
what I now make
up of it, I cannot see

more than hair
at first, a long
flowing hair there

fits it, faces
toward me as I
in it turn. Then

again pain,
for some reason, why
does it hurt. But

my feeling is,
this is what
you enjoy, so

twist to it while
the eye
of the other

face watches
me in pain. I
do not want what

I want. I dream it
in these two
painful things.

2

Why should she not
be attacked
literally. So

I attack my
mother, break
what I can reach,

the hair,
the thing I
came from.

3

If all women are
mothers, what
are men

standing
in dreams, mine
or theirs,

empty of
all but themselves.
They are so

lonely, unknown
there, I run
for whatever

is not
them, turning
into that consequence

makes me
my mother hating
myself.

4

In the day the
instruction is merely,
stand up. An

old joke relating
to the male
genital—up, up.

At night it
is the complex
as all things

are themselves and
their necessity,
even sexual. So

cunts and cocks
as eyes, noses, mouths,
have their objects:

hermaphrodite, one
sexed, bi-
sected in that lust.

5

What was the dream?
I have forgotten it
if I ever knew it

or dreamed
it more
than thinking. It

was to have been,
it was,
such I thought,

thinking. What
to dream, and what,
and what, to dream.

There was hair,
it hurt, I felt
the pain. I felt I did.

I will not
change into any-
thing you don't

like if
you will stay
with me as you said

you would. Don't
go. Away.
If this is where we are.

One Way

Of the two, one
faces one. In
the air there is

no tremor, no
odor. There is
a house around them,

of wood, of walls.
The mark is silence.
Everything hangs.

As he raises
his hand to
not strike her, as

again his hand
is raised, she has
gone, into another

room. In the room
left by her, he
cannot see himself

as in a mirror, as
a feeling of reflection.
He thinks he thinks,

of something else.
All the locked time,
all the letting go

down into it, as a
locked room, come to.
This time not changed,

but the way of feeling
secured by walls and books,
a picture hanging down,

a center shifted, dust
on all he puts his hand on,
disorder, papers and letters

and accumulations of clothing,
and bedclothes, and under his
feet the rug bunches.

Some Afternoon

Why not ride
with pleasure
and take oneself
as measure,

making the world
tacit description
of what's taken
from it

for no good reason,
the fact only.
There is a world
elsewhere, but here

the tangible faces
smile, breaking
into tangible pieces.
I see

myself and family,
and friends, and
animals attached,
the house, the road,

all go forward
in a huge
flash, shaken
with that act.

Goodbye, goodbye.
Nothing left
after the initial
blast but

some echo like this.
Only the faded
pieces of paper
etc.

Anger

1

The time is.
The air seems a cover,
the room is quiet.

She moves, she
had moved. He
heard her.

The children
sleep, the dog fed,
the house around them

is open, descriptive,
a truck through the walls,
lights bright there,

glaring, the sudden
roar of its motor, all
familiar impact

as it passed
so close. He
hated it.   `

But what does she answer.
She moves
away from it.

In all they save,
in the way of his saving
the clutter, the accumulation

of the expected disorder—
as if each dirtiness,
each blot, blurred

happily, gave
purpose, happily—
she is not enough there.

He is angry. His
face grows—as if
a moon rose

of black light,
convulsively darkening,
as if life were black.

It is black.
It is an open
hole of horror, of

nothing as if not
enough there is
nothing. A pit—

which he recognizes,
familiar, sees
the use in, a hole

for anger and
fills it
with himself,

yet watches on
the edge of it,
as if she were

not to be pulled in,
a hand could
stop him. Then

as the shouting
grows and grows
louder and louder

with spaces
of the same open
silence, the darkness,

in and out, him-
self between them,
stands empty and

holding out his
hands to both,
now screaming

it cannot be
the same, she
waits in the one

while the other
moans in the hole
in the floor, in the wall.

2

Is there some odor
which is anger,

a face
which is rage.

I think I think
but find myself in it.

The pattern
is only resemblance.

I cannot see myself
but as what I see, an

object but a man,
with lust for forgiveness,

raging, from that vantage,
secure in the purpose,

double, split.
Is it merely intention,

a sign quickly adapted,
shifted to make

a horrible place
for self-satisfaction.

I rage.
I rage, I rage.

3

You did it,
and didn't want to,

and it was simple.
You were not involved,

even if your head was cut off,
or each finger

twisted
from its shape until it broke,

and you screamed too
with the other, in pleasure.

4

Face me,
in the dark,
my face. See me.

It is the cry
I hear all
my life, my own

voice, my
eye locked in
self sight, not

the world what
ever it is
but the close

breathing beside
me I reach out
for, feel as

warmth in
my hands then
returned. The rage

is what I
want, what
I cannot give

to myself, of
myself, in
the world.

5

After, what
is it—as if
the sun had

been wrong to return,
again. It was
another life, a

day, some
time gone, it
was done.

But also
the pleasure, the
opening

relief
even in what
was so hated.

6

All you say you want
to do to yourself you do
to someone else as yourself

and we sit between you
waiting for whatever will
be at last the real end of you.

Distance

1

Hadn't I been
aching, for you,
seeing the

light there, such
shape as
it makes.

The bodies
fall, have
fallen, open.

Isn't it such
a form one
wants, the warmth

as sun
light on you.
But what

were you, where,
one thought, I
was always

thinking. The
mind itself,
impulse, of form

last realized,
nothing
otherwise but

a stumbling
looking after, a
picture

of light through
dust on
an indeterminate distance,

which throws
a radiator into
edges, shining,

the woman's long
length, the move-
ment of the

child, on her,
their legs
from behind.

2

Eyes,
days and
forms' photograph,

glazed
eyes, dear
hands. We

are walking,
I have
a face grown

hairy
and old, it
has greyed

to white
on the sides
of my cheeks. Stepping

out of
the car with these
endless people,

where are
you, am I happy,
is this car

mine. Another
life comes to
its presence,

here, you
sluffing, beside
me, me off, my-

self's warmth
gone inward,
a stepping

car, walking
waters on, such
a place like the

size of great
breasts, warmth and
moisture, come

forward, waking
to that edge
of the silence.

3

The falling back
from as in
love, or

casual friend-
ship, "I am so
happy, to

meet you—" These
meetings, it is
meet

we right (write)
to one another,
the slip-

shod, half-
felt, heart's
uneasinesses in

particular
forms, waking to
a body felt

as a hand pushed
between the long
legs. Is this

only the form,
"Your face
is unknown to me

but the hair, the
springing hair there
despite the rift,

the cleft,
between us, is
known, my own—"

What have *they*
done to me, who
are they coming

to me on such
informed feet, with
such substance of forms,

pushing
the flesh aside,
step in-

to my own,
my longing
for them.

II

Some Place

I resolved it, I
found in my life a
center and secured it.

It is the house,
trees beyond, a term
of view encasing it.

The weather
reaches only as some
wind, a little

deadened sighing. And
if the life weren't?
when was something to

happen, had I secured
that—had I, *had*
I, insistent.

There is nothing I am,
nothing not. A place
between, I am. I am

more than thought, less
than thought. A house
with winds, but a distance

—something loose in the wind,
feeling weather as that life,
walks toward the lights he left.

Song

I wouldn't
embarrass you
ever.

If there were
not place
or time for it,

I would go,
go elsewhere,
remembering.

I would
sit in a
flower, a face, not

to embarrass
you, would
be unhappy

quietly, would
never
make a noise.

Simpler,
simpler you
deal with me.

Song

What do you
want, love. To be
loved. What,

what wanted,
love, wanted
so much as love

like nothing
considered, no
feeling but

a simple
recognition
forgotten sits

in its feeling,
two things,
one and one.

For Helen

       . . . If I can
remember anything, it
is the way ahead
you made for me, specifically:

     wet-
ness, now the grass
as early it
has webs, all the lawn
stretched out from
the door, the back
one with a small crabbed
porch. The trees
are, then, so high,
a huge encrusted
sense of grooved trunk,
I can
slide my finger along
each edge.

A Night Sky

All the grass
dies
in front of us.

The fire
again
flares out.

The night
such a large
place. Stars

the points
but like
places no

depth, I see
a flat—
a plain as if the

desert
were showing smaller
places.

The Answer

Will we speak to each other
making the grass bend as if
a wind were before us, will our

way be as graceful, as
substantial as the movement
of something moving so gently.

We break things in pieces like
walls we break ourselves into
hearing them fall just to hear it.

Dimensions

1

Little places as
size of
one hand, shrink

to one finger
as tall
as, I am

sitting
down even
smaller.

2

Think if
understanding is
what you
had thought

of it, in
it you think
a picture
comes and

goes, re-
flected there
large faces
float but

no harm comes
to the sleeping
princess
ever.

3

My voice is
a foot. My
head is

a foot. I
club
people in

my mind, I
push them this
way, that

way, from
the little
way

I see them
up
the length,

for fear
of being hurt
they fall.

A Place

The wetness of that street, the light,
the way the clouds were heavy is
not description. But in the memory I fear

the distortion. I do not feel
what it was I was feeling. I am impatient to begin again, open

whatever door it was, find the weather
is out there, grey, the rain then and
now falling from the sky to the wet ground.

Some Echoes

Some echoes,
little pieces,
falling, a dust,

sunlight, by
the window, in
the eyes. Your

hair as
you brush
it, the light

behind
the eyes,
what is left of it.

Fancy

Do you know what
the truth is,
what's rightly
or wrongly said,

what is wiseness,
or rightness, what
wrong, or well-
done if it is,

or is not, done.
I thought.
I thought and
thought and thought.

In a place
I was sitting,
and there
it was, a little

faint thing
hardly felt, a
kind of small
nothing.

The World

I wanted so ably
to reassure you, I wanted
the man you took to be me,

to comfort you, and got
up, and went to the window,
pushed back, as you asked me to,

the curtain, to see
the outline of the trees
in the night outside.

The light, love,
the light we felt then,
greyly, was it, that

came in, on us, not
merely my hands or yours,
or a wetness so comfortable,

but in the dark then
as you slept, the grey
figure came so close

and leaned over,
between us, as you
slept, restless, and

my own face had to
see it, and be seen by it,
the man it was, your

grey lost tired bewildered
brother, unused, untaken—
hated by love, and dead,

but not dead, for an
instant, saw me, myself
the intruder, as he was not.

I tried to say, it is
all right, she is
happy, you are no longer

needed. I said,
he is dead, and he
went as you shifted

and woke, at first afraid,
then knew by my own knowing
what had happened—

and the light then
of the sun coming
for another morning
in the world.

Going

There is nothing
to turn from,
or to, no

way other
than forward, such
place as I mark

time. Let me
leave here a
mark, a

way through
her mind.

The City

Not from that
could you get it,
nor can things
comprise a form

just to be made.
Again, let
each be this or
that, they, together,

are many whereas,
one by one,
each is a wooden
or metal or even

water, or vegetable,
flower, a crazy orange
sun, a windy
dirt, and here is

a place to sit
shaded by tall buildings
and a bed that
grows leaves on

all its branches
which are
boards I know
soon enough.

Words

You are always
with me,
there is never
a separate

place. But if
in the twisted
place I
cannot speak,

not indulgence
or fear only,
but a tongue
rotten with what

it tastes— There is
a memory
of water, of
food, when hungry.

Some day
will not be
this one, then
to say

words like a
clear, fine
ash sifts,
like dust,

from nowhere.

A Reason

Each gesture
is a common one, a
black dog, crying, a
man, crying.

All alike, people
or things grow
fixed with what
happens to them.

I throw a stone.
It hits the wall,
it hits a dog,
it hits a child—

my sentimental
names for years
and years ago, from
something I've not become.

If I look
in the mirror,
the wall, I
see myself.

If I try
to do better
and better, I
do the same thing.

Let me hit you.
Will it hurt.
Your face is hurt
all the same.

The Shame

What will
the shame be,
what
cost to pay.

We are walking
in a wood,
wood of stones,
boulders for trees.

The sky
is a black
sudden cloud,
a sun.

Speak
to me, say
what things
were forgotten.

The Statue

I propose to you
a body bleached, a body
which would be dead
were it not alive.

We will stand it up
in the garden, which
we have taken such pains
to water. All the flowers

will grow at its feet,
and evenings it will
soften there as the darkness
comes down from such space.

Perhaps small sounds
will come from it, perhaps
the wind only, but its
mouth, could one see it,

will flutter. There will be
a day it walks just before
we come to look at it, but by then
it will have returned to its place.

The Window

There will be no simple
way to avoid what
confronts me. Again and
again I know it, but

take heart, hopefully,
in the world unavoidably
present. Here, I think,
is a day, not *a*
but *the*. My hands are

shaking, there is
an insistent tremble
from the night's
drinking. But what

was I after, you
were surely open to me.
Out the far window
there was such intensity

of yellow light. But love,
love I so wanted I
got, didn't I, and then
fell senseless, with relief.

To Bobbie

What can occur
invests the weather, also,
but the trees, again,
are in bloom.

The day will not
be less than that. I
am writing to you,
wishing to be rid of

these confusions. You
have so largely
let me continue, not
as indulgence but

then to say I
have said, and will,
anything is so
hard, at this moment.

In my mind, as
ever, you occur. Your
face is such
delight, I can

see the lines there
as the finest
mark of ourselves.
Your skin at moments

is translucent. I
want to make love
to you, now. The world
is the trees, you,

I cannot change it,
the weather
occurs, the mind
is not its only witness.

They

I wondered what had
happened to the chords.
There was a music,

they were following
a pattern. It was
an intention perhaps.

No field
but they walk
in it. No place

without them, any
discretion is useless.
They want a time, they

have a time, each
one in his place, an
endless arrival.

A Method

Patterns
of sounds, endless
discretions, whole
pauses of nouns,

clusters. This
and that, that
one, this
and that. Looking,

seeing, some
thing, being
some. A piece

of cake upon,
a face, a fact, that
description like
as if then.

A Sight

Quicker
than that, can't
get off "the
dead center of"

myself. *He*/*I*
were walking. Then
the place *is*/*was*
not ever enough. But

the house, if
admitted, were
a curiously wrought
complexity of flesh.

The eyes
windows, the head
roof form with
stubbornly placed

bricks of chimney.
I can remember, I
can. Then when
she first touched me,

when we were
lying in that bed,
was the feeling of
falling into no

matter we both lay
quiet, where
was it. I
felt her flesh

enclose mine. *Cock*,
they say, *prick*, *dick*,
I put it in her,
I lay there.

Come back, breasts,
come. Back. The sudden
thing of being
no one. I

never felt guilty,
I was confused but
could not feel
wrong, about it.

I wanted to kill her.
I tried it, tentatively,
just a little
hurt. Hurt me.

So immense she was.
All the day
lying flat, lying it seemed
upon a salty sea, the houses

bobbing
around her, under
her, I hung on
for dear life to her.

But when
now I walk, when
the day comes
to trees and a road,

where
is she. Oh, on my
hands and knees, crawl-
ing forward.

Pieces

I didn't
want
to hurt you.
Don't

stop
to think. It
hurts
to live

like this,
meat
sliced
walking.

The Circle

Houses in
the ring
to pass through,
past the

accumulated
sense of them,
I know
everyone.

I am
stumbling, my
feet are
awkwardly placed.

The man
who says
hello to me
is another

man, another
comes then. One
by one
the women who

look
after. In-
side the
thinking.

The Hole

There is
a silence
to fill. A
foot, a fit,

fall,
filled. If
you are
not careful all

the water spills.
One day
at the lake I took
off my bathing
suit

in the water,
peed
with pleasure, all
out, all

the water. Wipe
yourself, into
the tight
ass paper is pushed. Fatty

Arbuckle, the one
hero of the school,
took a coke bottle,
pushed it up his girl.

But I
wouldn't dare,
later,
felt there,

opened
myself.
Broken glass,
broken silence,

filled with screaming,
on the bed
she didn't want
it, but said, after,

the only time
it felt right. Was
I to force
her. Mother,

sister, once
seen, had breasts.
My father
I can't remember

but a man
in some building,
we were all swimming,
took out his

to piss, it
was large. He was
the teacher.
Everywhere

there is pleasure,
deep,
with hands
and feet.

I want
to, now I
can't wait any
longer. Talk

to me, fill
emptiness with
you, empty
hole.

A Prayer

Bless
something small
but infinite
and quiet.

There are senses
make an object
in their simple
feeling for one.

The Flower

Remember the way you
hunched up the first
times in bed, all your
body as you walked

seemed centered
in your breasts. It
was watching the world
come toward me, I felt

so alive and honored.
Me—least of all possibilities,
yet in bed before you,
the patient flower.

Same

Why am I
the laggard, as if
broken charms
were debris only.

Some thought
of it, broken
watch spring—
is not rusted merely.

That is all
they talk of
in Madrid, as much
to say the same.

The same thing
said the same
place is
the same.

Left in pieces,
objectively—
putting it
back together.

There

A place so
hostile it does

not want
any more, not

even not wanting,
is there.

Would one walk
or run, or avoid,

whatever—at
that moment

a voice
so tense

trying to
be acknowledged.

Joy

I could look at
an empty hole for hours
thinking it will
get something in it,

will collect
things. There is
an infinite emptiness
placed there.

A Picture

A little
house with
small
windows,

a gentle
fall of the
ground to
a small

stream. The trees
are both close
and green, a tall
sense of enclosure.

There is a sky
of blue
and a faint sun
through clouds.

A Piece

One and
one, two,
three.

The Box

for John Chamberlain

Three sides,
four
windows. Four

doors, three
hands.

Water Music

The words are a beautiful music.
The words bounce like in water.

Water music,
loud in the clearing

off the boats,
birds, leaves.

They look for a place
to sit and eat—

no meaning,
no point.

They (2)

They were trying to catch up.
But from the distance

between them, one thought
it would be a long time

even with persistent
running. They were walking

slower and slower
for hours and hours.

Was

The face
was
beautiful.

She was
a pleasure.
She

tried
to please.

The Farm

Tips of celery,
clouds of

grass—one
day I'll go away.

Indians

Big, wise
man. The happy
woman

in a place
she found. He
waited

in the clearing.

Enough

1

It is possible, in words, to speak
of what has happened—a sense

of there and here, now
and then. It is some other

way of being, prized enough,
that it makes a common

ground. Once
you were

alone and I
met you. It was late

at night.
I never

left after that,
not to my own mind,

but stayed
and stayed. Years

went by. What
were they. Days—

some happy
but some bitter

and sad. If I walked
across the room, then,

and saw you un-
expected, saw the particular

whiteness of
your body, a little

older, more
tired—in words

I possessed it, in
my mind I thought, and

you never knew
it, there I danced

for you, stumbling, in
the corner of my eye.

2

Don't we dance
a little bit,

slowly,
slowly. My

legs
will work

to the tunes of
a happy time.

3

A distance
separates, ob-

jectively, as from
shore, water, an

island projected,
up, against

the sun, a smoke
haze, drifting,

reflects
the golden city

now. Your
head and hands,

your eyes once
in words were

lakes but
this is an ocean

of vagueness. The sun
goes out. I

try to feel
where you are.

4

Hoo, hoo—
laughter.

Hoo, hoo—
laughter.

Obscene
distance. The

mind makes
its own

forms, looks
into its terror

so
selfishly

alone. Such
a fact so simply

managed there is
no need for any

one else. All
by myself I see

the obscene bodies
twisting, twisting,

my hand
explores their

delight, un-
noticed, my body

shrinks
back.

5

One
by one
the form

comes. One
thing follows
another. One

and one,
and one. Make
a picture

for the world
to be. It
will be.

6

You
there, me

here, or is it
me

there, you
here—there

or there
or here—and here.

In two
places, in two

pieces
I think.

7

Your body is a garbage can.
Your body is white, why

let others touch it, why
not. Why

my body so
tentative, do I

like the pain
of such impossible understanding.

Your body
is a white

softness, it has
its own

place time
after time.

8

I vow to my life to respect it.
I will not wreck it.

I vow to yours to be
enough, enough, enough.

Here

What
has happened
makes

the world.
Live
on the edge,

looking.

Intervals

Who
am I—
identity
singing.

Place
a lake
on ground, water
finds a form.

Smoke
on the air
goes higher
to fade.

Sun bright,
trees dark green,
a little movement
in the leaves.

Birds singing
measure distance,
intervals between
echo silence.

Water (2)

Water drips,
a fissure of leaking
moisture spills
itself unnoticed.

What
was I looking at,
not to see
that wetness spread.

The Eye

The eye I look out of
or hands I use,
feet walking,
they stay particular.

I wanted
one place to be
where I was
always.

I wanted you
somehow equal,
my love, one says—
I speak with that body.

But then it happens—
another time, a particular
circumstance—surrounded by such
a distance.

You took my heart
which was with you,
you took my hands
which I used for you.

Oh when regrets stop
and the silence comes
back to be
a place still for us,

our bodies will tell
their own story, past
all error,
come back to us.

Of Years

Of a few years
come into focus—
peace and understanding,
the uneasy virtues.

Of a mist.
A night's peace
waking to sullenness,
uneasy companion—

of force,
of coercion, compulsion,
of nagging, insistent
suspicion.

Of nothing
more than a moment.
Sudden candle light
shattered the night.

Song

How simply
    for another
pace the virtues,
    peace and goodwill.

Sing pleasure,
    the window's opening,
unseen back of it
    the door closes.

How peace, how happiness,
    locked as insistence,
force weather, see sun,
    and won't look back.

For Joel

Some simple
virtue of silence
you taught me once,
not to talk too much.

In your place, waiting,
up all night, talking
and drinking, flowers
for your wife then—

but not accepted.
The test was
how much unhappiness
either one of us could endure.

I think of friends,
some known for years.
There are men
made sense for me.

Measures—
ways of being in one's life,
happy or unhappy,
never dead to it.

Joy to the marriage, now,
of such a friend
gave me such reassurance
in his own pain,

joy to strength and weakness,
to what won't go dead
to its own pleasure
but likes to laugh.

A full shout
for happiness, a
bride of such delight,
a groom so wise.

A Birthday

Shall we address it
as you, lovely one,
singing those intervals

of a complex
loneliness, a wanting too
to know

its condition. Together
is one by one,
and a beauty

comes of it, a substance
of beauty—beauty, *beauty*—
dripping its condition.

I had thought
a moment of stasis
possible, some

thing fixed—
days, worlds—
but what I know

is water, as you
are water, as you
taught me water

is wet. Now slowly
spaces occur, a ground is
disclosed as dirt. The

mountains come of it,
the sky precedes, and where
there had been only

land now sticks and stones
are evident. So we are
here, so we are.

Dancing

To be dancer
of my own dismay,
to let my legs and arms
move in their own feeling,

I make a form of assumptions
as real as clothes on a line,
a car moving
that sees another coming,

dancing as all would
were it not for what it thought
it was always doing,
or could leave

itself to itself
whatever it is, dancing,
or better, a jerking leap
toward impulse.

A Tally

A tally of forces, consequent
memories, of times and places—
habits of preparation at other
points of time and place.

And the hand found the fingers
still on it, moved the thumb,
easily, to the forefinger,
still worked. What

has come. Age? But,
to know itself, needs
occasion, as, no longer young
wants a measure.

The mirror the mind is,
reflective, in that guise,
long habit of much delaying thought
to savor terms of the impression—

it's not as bad as one thought,
but that is relative. Not as simple
as the boat is leaking, he, she, it,
they—or we, you and I, are sinking.

Within the world, this one, many quirks
accomplished, effected, in the thought,
I don't know how, I only live here,
with the body I walk in.

Hence I love you, I did, do,
a moment ago it was daylight,
now dark I wonder what the memory means,
loving you more than I had thought to.

No agreement to stay, see it out,
the dereliction of fleshy duties—
but not burn down the house
for whatever rage was once.

"Oh My Love . . ."

Oh my love,
in other times
the things we are
were beauty too.

In ways that were
I never knew
were possible
might talk to you.

Or on and on
and up and down
seasons and days
might make a place

unlike such
awkwardness makes
this one awkward
fall apart.

Fragments

Decorous, and forbearing further correction,
to the empty halls he announces
pardon. No wound deeper than
death, he says, not knowing.

.

The fall of
feet dancing
to sounds within
his hearing. Oh,
how much he heard.

.

Little song, sing
days of happiness. Make
a pardonable wonder
of one's blunders.

Pieces

yes, yes,
       that's what
I wanted,
       I always wanted,
I always wanted,
       to return
to the body
       where I was born.

ALLEN GINSBERG
Song

As REAL as thinking
wonders created
by the possibility—

forms. A period
at the end of a sentence
which

began *it was*
into a present,
a presence

saying
something
as it goes.

•

No forms less
than activity.

All words—
days—or
eyes—

or happening
is an event only
for the observer?

No one
there. Everyone
here.

•

Small facts
of eyes, hair
blonde, face

looking like a
flat painted
board. How

opaque as if
a reflection
merely, skin

vague glove of
randomly seen
colors.

      •

Inside
and out

impossible
locations—

reaching in
from out-

side, out
from in-

side—as
middle:

one
hand.

Flowers

No knowledge rightly understood
can deprive us of the mirth of flowers.
EDWARD DAHLBERG

No thing less than one thing
or more—

no sun
but sun—

or water
but wetness found—

What truth is it
that makes men so miserable?

Days we die
are particular—

This life cannot be lived
apart from what it must forgive.

The Family

Father
and mother
and sister
and sister
and sister.

•

Here we are.
There are five
ways to say this.

Kate's

If I were you
and you were me
I bet you'd
do it too.

For You

Like watching rings extend in water
this time of life.

A Step

Things
         come and go.
Then
         let them.

HAVING TO –
what do I think
to say now.

Nothing but
comes and goes
in a moment.

         •

Cup.
Bowl.
Saucer.
Full.

         •

The way into the form,
the way out of the room—

The door, the hat,
the chair, the fact.

         •

Sitting, waves on the beach,
or else clouds, in the sky,

a road, going by,
cars, a truck, animals, in crowds.

THE CAR
moving
the hill
down

which yellow
leaves
light forms
declare.

•

Car coughing moves with
a jerked energy forward.

•

Sit. Eat
a doughnut.

Love's consistency
favors me.

•

A big crow on the
top of the tree's
form more stripped
with leaves gone
overweights it.

PIECES OF CAKE crumbling
in the hand trying to hold
them together to give each
of the seated guests a piece.

•

Willow, the house, an egg—
what do they make?

Hat, happy, a door—
what more.

The Finger

Either in or out of
the mind, a conception
overrides it. *So that*
that time I was a stranger,

bearded, with clothes that were
old and torn. I was told,
it was known to me, my
fate would be timeless. Again

and again I was to
get it right, the story I
myself knew only the way of,
but the purpose if it

had one, was not mine.
The quiet shatter of the light,
the image folded into
endlessly opening patterns—

had they faced me into
the light so that my
eye was blinded? At moments
I knew they had gone but

searched for her face, the pureness
of its beauty, the endlessly sensual—
but no sense as that now reports it.
Rather, she was beauty, that

Aphrodite I had known of,
and caught sight of as *maid*—
a girlish openness—or known
as a woman turned from the light.

I knew, however, the other,
perhaps even more. She was there
in the room's corner, as she would be,
bent by a wind it seemed

would never stop blowing,
braced like a seabird,
with those endlessly clear grey eyes.
Name her, Athena—what name.

The osprey, the sea, the waves.
To go on telling the story,
to go on though no one hears it,
to the end of my days?

Mercury, Hermes, in dark glasses.
Talk to him—but as if
one talked to the telephone,
telling it to please listen—

is that right, have I said it—
and the reflecting face echoes
some cast of words in mind's eye,
attention a whip of surmise.

And the power to tell
is glory. One unto one
unto one. And though all
mistake it, it is one.

I saw the stones thrown
at her. I felt a radiance transform
my hands and my face.
I blessed her, I was one.

Are there other times?
Is she that woman,
or this one. Am I the man—
and what transforms.

Sit by the fire.
I'll dance a jig I learned
long before we were born
for you and you only then.

I was not to go
as if to somewhere,
was not in the mind
as thinking knows it,

but danced in a jigging
intensive circle
before the fire and its heat
and that woman lounging.

How had she turned herself?
She was largely warm—
flesh heavy—and smiled
in some deepening knowledge.

There are charms.
The pedlar and the small dog
following and the whistled,
insistent song.

I had the pack,
the tattered clothing,
was neither a man nor not one,
all that—

and who was she,
with the fire behind her,
in the mess of that place,
the dust, the scattered pieces,

her skin so warm,
so massive, so stolid in her
smiling the charm did not
move her but rather

kept her half-sleepy attention,
yawning, indulging the manny
who jiggled a world before her
made of his mind.

She was young,
she was old,
she was small.
She was tall with

extraordinary grace. Her face
was all distance, her eyes
the depth of all one had thought of,
again and again and again.

To approach, to hold her,
was not possible.
She laughed and turned
and the heavy folds of cloth

parted. The nakedness
burned. Her heavy breath,
her ugliness, her lust—
but her laughing, her low

chuckling laugh, the way
she moved her hand to the
naked breast, then to
her belly, her hand with its fingers.

Then *shone* —
and whatever is said
in the world, or forgotten,
or not said, makes a form.

The choice is simply,
I will—as mind is a finger,
pointing, as wonder
a place to be.

Listen to me, let
me touch you
there. You are young again,
and you are looking at me.

Was there ever
such foolishness more
than what thinks it knows
and cannot see, was there ever

more? Was the truth
behind us, or before?
Was it one
or two, and who was I?

She was laughing, she was
laughing, at me,
and I danced, and
I danced.

Lovely, lovely woman, let
me sing, *one to*
one to one, and let
me follow.

ONE THING
done, the
rest follows.

            •

Not from not
but in in.

            •

Here here
here. Here.

I CANNOT see you
there for what you
thought you were.

The faded memories
myself enclose
passing too.

     •

Were you there
or here now—
such a slight sound
what was your step makes.

     •

Here I
am. There
you are.

     •

The head
of a
pin on . . .

     •

Again
and again
now
also.

Gemini

Two eyes, two hands—
in one two are given.

The words
are messages

from another,
not understood but given.

     •

Neither one, nor the other,
nor of a brother—but in

the one, two, restless,
confined to a place ruled

by a moon, and another one
with messages, rather, sequences

of words that are not to be understood
but somehow given to a world.

All this dances in a room,
two by two, but alone.

.

From one to two,
is the first rule.

Of two minds the twin
is to double life given.

.

What it says is that one
is two, the twin,

that the messenger comes
to either, that these fight

to possess, but do not
understand—that if the

moon rules, there is
"domestic harmony"—but if the blood

cry, the split so divide,
there can be no

company for the two in one.
He is alone.

IN SECRET
the out's in—

the wise
surprised, all

going coming,
begun undone.

Hence the fool dances
in endless happiness.

.

A circling with
snake-tail in mouth—

what the head was
looked *forward*,

what backward is,
then guess.

Either way,
it will stay.

"Time" is some sort of hindsight, or else rhythm of activity—e.g., now it's 11 days later—"also alive" like they say.

.

Where it is
was and
will be never
only here.

.

—fluttering as
falling, leaves,
knives, to
avoid—tunnel
down the
vague sides . . .

.

—it
it—

"Follow the Drinking Gourd . . ."

Present again
present present
again present
present again

leaves falling,
knives, a windspout
of nostalgic faces,
into the air.

Car glides forward.
Drive from Bloomington,
Indiana to Lexington,
Ky. Here the walls

of fall, the stone,
the hill, the trucks
in front with
the unseen drivers.

Stoney Lonesome. Gnaw-
bone. A house
sits back from
the road.

A Christmas
present—all
present and ac-
counted for? Sir?

Passage of time.
The sun shone level
from the left-
hand side of

the land—a flat-
seeming distance,
left, east? South?
Sun shines.

Go on. Tell
me, them, him,
her, their
apparent forms.

The "present dented,"
call it "long
distance," come
here home. Then

a scarecrow there, here a
snowman. Where in
the world then an-
other place?

Drive on
what seems an
exceptionally smooth
and even surface,

the forward cars
way up there glint
in that sun of
a universe of mine.

And for twenty eight
dollars—all this.
All in the mind
in time, in place—

what it costs to rent
agency? Give
me a present, your
hand to help

me understand this.
So far, so long,
so anywhere a
place if not this

one—driving,
screaming a lovely
song perhaps, or
a cigar smoke—

"When they were
young in Kentucky
a man to freedom
took them in a cave . . ."

A famous song,
to drive to,
sing along the
passing way—

or *done* or
right or
wrong or
wander on.

The Moon

Earlier in the evening the moon
was clear to the east,
over the snow of the yard
and fields—a lovely

bright clarity and perfect
roundness, isolate,
riding as they say the
black sky. Then we went

about our businesses of the
evening, eating supper, talking,
watching television, then
going to bed, making love,

and then to sleep. But before
we did I asked her to look
out the window at the moon
now straight up, so that

she bent her head and looked
sharply up, to see it.
Through the night it must
have shone on, in that

fact of things—another
moon, another night—a
full moon in the winter's
space, a white loneliness.

I came awake to the blue
white light in the darkness,
and felt as if someone
were there, waiting, alone.

Numbers

For Robert Indiana

ONE

What
singular upright flourishing
condition . . .
it enters here,
it returns here.

    •

Who was I that
thought it was
another one by
itself divided or multiplied
produces one.

    •

This time, this
place, this
one.

     •

You are not
me, nor I you.

     •

All ways.

     •

As of a stick,
stone, some-

thing so
fixed it has

a head, walks,
talks, leads

a life.

TWO

When they were
first made, all the
earth must have
been their reflected
bodies, for a moment—
a flood of seeming
bent for a moment back
to the water's glimmering—
how lovely they came.

     •

What you wanted
I felt, or felt I felt.
This was more than one.

     •

This point of so-called
consciousness is forever
a word making up
this world of more
or less than it is.

•

Don't leave me.
Love me. One by one.

•

As if to sit
by me were another
who did sit. So

to make you
mine, in the mind,
to know you.

THREE

They come now with
one in the middle—
either side thus
another. Do they

know who each other
is or simply walk
with this pivot between them.
Here forms have possibility.

•

When either this
or that becomes
choice, this fact

of things enters.
What had been
agreed now

alters to
two and one,
all ways.

        •

The first
triangle, of form,
of people,

sounded a
lonely occasion I
think—the

circle begins
here, intangible—
yet a birth.

FOUR

This number for me
is comfort, a secure
fact of things. The

table stands on
all fours. The dog
walks comfortably,

and two by two
is not an army
but friends who love

one another. Four
is a square,
or peaceful circle,

celebrating return,
reunion,
love's triumph.

        •

The card which is the
four of hearts must
mean enduring experience
of life. What other
meaning could it have.

⋅

Is a door
four—but
who enters.

⋅

Abstract—yes, as
two and two
things, four things—
one and three.

FIVE

Two by
two with
now another

in the middle
or else at
the side.

⋅

From each
of the four
corners draw

a line to
the alternate
points. Where

these intersect
will be
five.

⋅

When younger this was
a number used to
count with, and

to imagine a useful
group. Somehow the extra
one—what is more than four—

reassured me there would be
enough. Twos and threes or
one and four is plenty.

•

A way to draw stars.

SIX

Twisting
    as forms of it
two and three—

    on the sixth
day had finished
    all creation—

hence holy—
    or that the sun
is "furthest from

    equator & appears
to pause, before
    returning . . ."

or that it "contains
    the first even number
(2), and the first odd

    number (3), the former representing
the male member, and the latter
    the *muliebris pudenda* . . ."

Or two triangles interlocked.

SEVEN

We are seven, echoes in
my head like a nightmare of
responsibility—seven
days in the week, seven
years for the itch of
unequivocal involvement.

•

Look
at
the
light
of
this
hour.

•

I was born at seven in
the morning and my
father had a monument
of stone, a pillar, put
at the entrance of the
hospital, of which he was head.

•

*At sixes
and sevens*—the pen
lost, the paper:

a night's dead
drunkenness. Why
the death of something now

so near if *this*
number is holy.
Are all

numbers one?
Is counting forever
beginning again.

•

Let this be the end of the seven.

Say "eight"—
be patient.

Two fours
show the way.

•

Only this number
marks the cycle—

the eight year interval—
for that confluence

makes the full moon shine
on the longest

or shortest
day of the year.

•

Now summer fades.
August its month—
this interval.

•

She is eight
years old, holds
a kitten, and
looks out at me.

•

Where are you.
One table.
One chair.

            •

In light lines count the interval.
Eight makes the time wait quietly.

            •

No going back—
though half is
four and
half again
is two.

            •

Oct-
ag-
on-
al.

NINE

There is no point
of rest here.
It wavers,

it reflects multiply
the *three*
times three.

Like a mirror
it returns here
by being there.

            •

Perhaps in the
emphasis implicit—
over and over—

"triad of triads,"
"triply sacred and perfect
number"—that

resolves what—
in the shifting,
fading containment?

·

Somehow the game
where a nutshell covers
the one object, a

stone or coin, and
the hand is
quicker than the eye—

how is that *nine*,
and not *three*
chances, except that

three imaginations of it
might be, and there are
two who play—

making six, but
the world is real also,
in itself.

·

More. The nine months
of waiting that discover
life or death—

another life or death—
not yours, not
mine, as we watch.

·

The serial diminish-
ment or progression of
the products which

helped me remember:
nine times two is one-eight
          nine times nine is eight-one—
at each end,

move forward, backward,
then, and the same
numbers will occur.

          •

What law
or
mystery

is involved
protects
itself.

ZERO

Where are you—who
          by not being here
are here, but here
          by not being here?

There is no trick to reality—
          a mind
makes it, any
          mind. You

walk the years in a
          nothing, a no
place I know as well as
          the last breath

I took, blowing the smoke
          out of a mouth
will also go nowhere,
          having found its way.

          •

Reading that primitive systems
seem to have natural cause for
the return to one, after ten—
but this is *not* ten—out of
nothing, one, to return to that—
Americans have a funny way—
somebody wrote a poem about it—
of "doing nothing"—What else
should, *can*, they do?

.

What
by being not
is—is not
by being.

.

When holes taste good
we'll put them in our bread

.

The Fool

"With light step, as if earth and its trammels had little
power to restrain him, a young man in gorgeous vestments
pauses at the brink of a precipice among the great heights of
the world; he surveys the blue distance before him—its expanse of sky rather than the prospect below. His act of eager
walking is still indicated, though he is stationary at the given
moment; his dog is still bounding. The edge which opens on
the depth has no terror; it is as if angels were waiting to up-
hold him, if it came about that he leaped from the height.
His countenance is full of intelligence and expectant dream.
He has a rose in one hand and in the other a costly wand,
from which depends over his right shoulder a wallet curiously embroidered. He is a prince of the other world on his
travels through this one—all amidst the morning glory, in the
keen air. The sun, which shines behind him, knows whence
he came, whither he is going, and how he will return by
another path after many days . . ."

THE BEDPOST is an
extraordinary shape
to have happened though
in nature this upthrust

with its conical cap and
bulging middle is met
with often enough. But the
bar, horizontal, joining

the two posts, I have not
seen this elsewhere except
as the cross bar of the collar
bone, my own, or those of others.

·

What she says she wants
she wants she says.

ONE/THE SUN/
Moon/one.

·

How far one has come
in these seven league boots.

·

The pen,
the lines it
leaves, forms
divine—nor
laugh nor giggle.
This prescription
is true.
Truth is a scrawl,
all told
in all.

·

Back where things were
sweeter, water falls
and thinks again.

•

Here, there,
every-
where.

•

Never write
to say more
than saying
something.

———————

Words
are
pleasure.
All
words.

•

Names

Harry has written
all he knows.
Miriam tells
her thought, Peter
says again
his mind. Robert and John,
William, Tom,
and Helen, Ethel,
that woman whose name
he can't remember
or she even him
says to tell
all they know.

CAN FEEL IT in the pushing,
not letting myself relax
for any reason, hanging on.

·

Thinking—and coincident
experience of the situation.

"I think he'll hit me."
He does. Etc.

·

Reflector/ -ive/ -ed.

·

Chicago

Say that you're
        lonely—and want
something to
        place you—

going around groping
        either by mind
or hand—but behind
        the pun is a

door you keep open,
        one way,
so they won't touch you
        and still let you stay.

·

I can't see in
        this place more
than the walls
        and door—
a light flat
        and air hot,
and drab, drab, drab
        and locked.

Would dying be here?
Never go anywhere you
        can't live.

Concrete blocks painted an "off white" yellow tone—institu-
tional—*very* noisy, senses of people next side of wall, etc.
Get *used* to shrinking space— They'll let you out when
there's reason.

PLEASURES of pain,
        oh lady,
fail in the argument—
        This way

of making friends
        you made me let
go of, losing myself
        in a simple fact.

                •

NYC—

    Streets as ever blocky, grey—square sense of rectangular
enclosures, emphasized by the coldness of the time of year,
and the rain. In moving in the cab—continual sense of small
(as size, i.e., all "cars," etc.) persistent difficulties.

        •

The Friends

I want to help you
by understanding what
you want me to
understand by saying so.

        •

I listen. I had
an ego once upon
a time—I do still,
for you listen to me.

Let's be very still.
Do you hear? Hear
what, I will say when-
ever you ask me to listen.

    •

I wouldn't joke about
your wife wanting to wash
her hair at eleven o'clock
at night but supposing she

wants to I'd consider her
thoughts on the matter equally
with yours wherever you were
and for whatever reason.

    •

Don't think I'm
so awful you can
afford my company
so as not to
put me down more.

    •

God, I hate
simplistic logic like—
I like it. Who cares.

    •

Liking is as
liking does
for you, for me.

    •

The "breathtaking banalities"
one only accomplishes in
retrospect. Hindsight—

they call it—like the
backend of a horse. *Horse's
ass*, would be the way.

Diction

The grand time when the words
were fit for human allegation,

and imagination of small, local
containments, and the lids fit.

What was the wind blew through it,
a veritable bonfire like they say—

and did say in hostile, little voices:
"It's changed, it's not the same!"

·

America

America, you ode for reality!
Give back the people you took.

Let the sun shine again
on the four corners of the world

you thought of first but do not
own, or keep like a convenience.

People are your own word, you
invented that locus and term.

Here, you said and say, is
where we are. Give back

what we are, these people you made,
us, and nowhere but you to be.

·

Citizen

Write a giggly ode about
        motherfuckers—Oedipus—
or Lysergic Acid—a word
        for an experience, verb

or noun. Count down, count
        Orlovsky, count up—
in the air, you filthy
        window washer. Why

not clean up the world.
        You need it, I
need it—more than
        either one of us can get.

        •

Place

Thinking of you asleep on a
        bed on a pillow, on a
        bed—the ground or space

you lie on. That's enough to
        talk to now I got space and
        time like a broken watch.

        •

Hello there—instant
reality on the other
end of this so-called line.

        •

Oh no you
don't, do you?

        •

Late, the words, late
the form of them, al-

ready past what they were
fit for, one and two and three.

•

The Puritan Ethos

Happy the man who loves what
he has and worked for it also.

•

There is a lake of clear water.
There are forms of things despite us.

Pope said, "a little learning,"
and, *and*, *and*, *and*—the same.

Why don't you go home and sleep
and come back and talk some more.

•

By location, e.g., where
or here—or what words in
time make of things. *Space*,
they say, and think a several

dimensioned locus. Mr.
Warner came from a small
town in the middle mid-
eastern Atlantic states.

That—in time—displaces
all else might be said of
him, or whatever became
of him in that other space he knew.

•

The Province

Trying to get "our men
     back" and "our ship
back"—"tactical
     nuclear weapons"—dig!

Shee-it. The *world*,
     dad, is where you
live unless you've for-
     gotten it through that

incredible means called
     efficacy *or* understanding
or superior lines of
     or, *or* something else.

     •

Canada

"The maple leaf forever"
     "in 1867—"
"inspired the world
     to say—"

HAPPY LOVE, this
agreement, coincidence
like crossing streets.

     •

Forms face
facts find.

     •

One cock
pheasant one
hen pheasant
walk along.

The Boy

Push yourself in on others
hard enough, they beat you
with sticks and whips—the birth

of love. E.g., affection aroused,
it moves to be close, touch, and
feel the warm livingness of an-

other, any other, sucked, stroked,
the club itself possibly a symbol of
the obvious. My mother had hair,

and when I grew older, so did
I, all over my face, which I wanted
to be there, and grew a beard henceforth.

3 in 1

for Charlotte

The bird
flies
out the
window. She
flies.

•

The bird flies
out the
window. She
flies.

•

The bird
flies. She
flies.

They

What could
they give me I
hadn't myself
discovered—

The *world*,—that
I'd fallen upon
in some
distracted drunkenness—

Or that the rules
were *wrong*, an
observation they
as well as I
knew now—

They were imagination
also. If they
would be as the
mind could see *them*,

then it all was
true and the
mind followed and
I also.

•

Echo

Yes but your sweetness
derives drunkenness—

over, and over, not
your face, not your

hand—no you nor
me is real now—

Nothing here now,
nothing there now.

        •

In this fact of face and body—looking out—a *kind* of pleasure. That is, no argument stops me. Not—"yes"—"no"—
gradually? Only involved as openings, sexual also, seem to
be—but is "no" my final way of speaking? E.g., *a* "poet" of
such impossibilities "I" makes up?

So TIRED
it falls
apart.

WHY SAY to them
truth is confounded with opposition,
or that—or *that* what is
were a happiness.

Simple, to be said, a life
is nothing more than itself,
and all the bodies together
are, one by one, the measure.

        •

I am finally
what I had to be,
neither more nor less—
become happiness.

FORMS' PASSAGE as
water beside the white
upright group of apparently
flat buildings—The river's

bend, seen from the sky—
down, under, with the eye.

•

Allen's saying as we fly out of NYC—the look of the city
underneath us like a cellular growth, "cancer"—so that
senses of men on the earth as an investment of it radiates a
world cancer—Burroughs' "law" finally quite clear.

•

Mississippi much as—pen blots with pressure (?)—the sky
ahead a faint light yellow—like "northern" lights. —Why the
goddamn impatience with that *as*—the damn function of *simile*, always a displacement of what *is* happening.

•

Life like you
think you have
it till it isn't
—but is, inevitably—
behind the scene.

DAYS LATER—neither having
become nor not become a
convenience to assumptions.

•

You look up the street to
the far bay and boats
floating in a sunny haze.

Either way, the streets lead
down, from this hill. An
apartment house of tiered

layers sits opposite on
the far corner. We get
into the car and drive off.

•

Nowhere one
goes will
one ever
be away
enough from
wherever
one was.

•

Falling-in windows—
the greenhouse back of
Curleys' house. The
Curleys were so good
to me, their mother
held me on her lap.

No CLOUDS out the window,
flat faint sky of faded blue.
The sun makes spring now,

a renewal possibly of like energy,
something forgotten almost remembered,
echoes in my mind like the grass.

•

Your opaqueness, at moments,
would be the mirror. Your
face closed as a door—

that insists on nothing,
but not to be entered—
wanting simply to be left alone.

I slept, it seemed, the moment
I lay down in the bed, even,
it might have been, impatient

to be out of it, gone away,
to what densities can be there
in a night's sleep, day by day.

But, all in the mind it comes
and goes. My own life is given
me back again, something forgotten.

                •

I want to sing.
What makes it
impossible—so

that one lifts
that dead bulk
with such insistent energy?

                •

"But now it's come to distances . . ."

                            —Leonard Cohen

                •

Thinking—a tacit, tactile distance between us at this moment—much as if we had lives in "different worlds"—which,
I suppose, would be the case despite all closeness otherwise,
i.e., almost as if the moment one were "thinking," and not
literally taking, finding place in something we both had occasion in, that this fact of things becomes a separation. I.e.,
it seems not possible to live the "same" life, no matter what
one wants, wills, or tries to have the so-called "case."—
Like old "romantic" self-query, come of obvious unrest and
frustration.

Echo Of

Can't myself
let off this
fiction. "You
don't exist,

baby, you're
dead." Walk
off, on—the
light bulb

overhead, beside,
or, the bed, you
think you laid
on? When, what.

　　•

The

The water
waiting far
off to the
east, the
west—the
shores of the world.

SITUATION OF feeling increasingly "apart" from people in
reading—and/or probably the fact of going *into* the reading
to find a place in the welter of randomness of people there—
or my assumption, in fatigue, that no one's making it.

　　•

You are all lovely,
hairy, scarey
people after all.

　　•

Again

One more day gone,
done, found in
the form of days.

It began, it
ended—was
forward, backward,

slow, fast, a
sun shone, clouds,
high in the air I was

for awhile with others,
then came down
on the ground again.

No moon. A room in
a hotel—to begin
again.

THE WHICH it
was, form
seen—there
here, re-
peated for/
as/—There
is a "parallel."

    •

When and/or if, as,—however, you do "speak" to people,
i.e., as condition of the circumstance (as Latin: "what's
around") a/n "im(in)pression." "I'll" *crush* you to "death"—
"flying home."

    •

Allen last night—context of *how* include the output of human function in an experience thereof makes the fact of it
become possibility of pleasure—not fear, not pain. Every-
body *spends* it (the "life" they inhabit) all—hence, no problem
of that kind, except (*large* fact) in imagination.

IN THE HOUSE of
old friend, whose
friend, my

friend, the trouble
with you, who,
he is, there, here,
we were *not*.

    •

The voice of the
echo of time, the
same—"I

know you," no
pain in that, we are
all around what we are.

    •

(Re Bob's film, CUT)

Pictures of the movement.
Pictures of the red-headed
man going down on—

pictures of the red-
haired man on the red-
headed girl on the—

pictures of the flat form
cutting hair off, the long,
the echoic scissors cutting.

    •

—Like problem of depth perception, each movement to the
familiarity (a 20 year "distance") confronts the time—as—
distance of the "real" event, i.e., *now*—but "here," as a habit,
is what we are lacking *here*.

P.S.

Thinking of Olson—"we are
as we find out we are."

Ice Cream

Sure,
Herbert—
Take a bite—

The crowd
milling on the bridge, the
night forms in

the air. So
much has gone
away.

.

Upside
down
forms
faces.

.

Letter to General
Eisenhower from

General
Mount-

batten.
Better

be
right.

Better batter
bigger pancakes.

You Chief
Eat It.

    •

Something that hasn't as yet had chance to
wants the possibility of asking

if what might be might be,
if what has to be is otherwise.

    •

Oh so cute in your
gorgeous gown you were.

You were, you were,
you-are-or-you-were-you-were.

WHAT
do you think it is.
Dogs wandering
the roads.

All I knew or know
began with this—
emptiness
with its incessant movement.

Where was it—
to be younger, older,
if not here,
if not there.

Calling,
calling over the shoulder,
through a mist,
to those fading people.

    •

This singleness
you make an evidence
has purpose.

You are not alone,
however one—not
so alone.

Light finds a place
you can see it in
such singleness.

·

There might be
an imaginary
place to be—
there might be.

·

Grey mist forms
out the window,
leaves showing green,
the dark trunks of trees—

place beyond?
The eye sees, the
head apparently records
the vision of these eyes.

What have I seen,
now see? There were
times before
I look now.

·

Re C—

Making a form for you
of something, a vehicle
of the head, round
wheel eyes for getting there.

Why do you get up so
restlessly if sitting down is
where I always find you—
after all these years.

You want to fight?
You want a black eye for
your troubles? How be
young and yet to be loved?

Sprightly, you have a
head I do put wheels on,
and two arms and two legs.
You'll travel.

LIKE A MAN committed to searching
out long darkened corridors with doors,
and only the spot of the flashlight to
be a way into and back out, to safety.

    •

Peace, brother, to all of it,
in all senses, in all places,
in every way, in all
senses, in all places, in
every way.

    •

Here now *you* are—
by what means?
And who to know it?

    •

A lady in a dress of velvet,
a girl in a cotton dress,
a woman, walking—
something like that, with hair—

some form you feel or
you said you felt was
like that the times we sat
and you told me what

to look for—this
fact of some woman
with some man like
that was really all.

    •

The sun will set again on
the edge of the sky or whatever

you want to call it. *Out there*,
not here, the sun "will set,

did set, is *now* setting."
Hear, goddamnit, hear.

    •

I have no ease
calling things beautiful
which are by that
so called to my mind.

    •

You want

the fact

of things

in words,

of words.

    •

Endless trouble, endless pleasure,
endless distance, endless ways.

    •

What do you want with the phone
if you won't answer it.

    •

Don't say it doesn't rhyme
if you won't read it—nor break the

line in pieces that goes
and goes and goes.

> •

Each moment constitutes reality,
or rather may constitute
reality, or may have *done*
so, or perhaps *will?*

I'd rather sit on my
hands on purpose, and be
an idiot—or just go off somewhere,
like they say, to something else.

> •

The News

Unresponsible
people versus

serious
people. In

New Brunswick
this is a problem.

> •

The language
of instruction
for their children . . .

> •

The English
speaking people
are not
a numerous group . . .

> •

Allentown
Arts Festival
Days . . .

late
film and
video tape
report . . .

    •

NIAGARA MOHAWK

SMELL OF gum wrappers as of Saturday afternoon at movies
in Maynard, Mass.—

Sudden openness of summer—everything seems to hang in
the air.

    •

I figure

if I eat so much,
I get so fat.

If I don't eat so much
I don't get so fat—

so,
so.

    •

Laugh at the domestic comedy,
the woman falls flat on her face,

the man staggers down the street,
the kid falls down, the dog dies.

Think of the implications,
what you could sell.

    •

"It's rare that the city of Buffalo
gets to shape its own destiny . . ."

·

Take advantage of this,
take advantage of what's downtown
and link the two with a
rapid transit system . . .

WHERE WE are there must
be something to place us.

Look around. What do you see
that you can recognize.

·

Anxious about the weather,
folding the door shut, unwrapping
the floor covering and rolling it
forward, at the door.

·

So that's what you do:
ask the same question
and keep answering.

·

Was that right.

THE DAY comes and goes,
the far vistas of the west
are piles of clouds and
an impending storm. I see
it all now—nothing more.

·

Love in a
car takes my
wife away from me.

She is busy. She thinks
in an activity and goes
about her own business.

    •

Love one.
Kiss two.

    •

In my own ego structure, have to find *place* for shift in imagination of experience—or else—more probably—walk as
ever, even sentimentally, straight ahead. In age of hanging
gardens variety, now,—all possible, either way—and times
insist on "no problems." That way, so to speak, there never
was.—One wants *one*.

> "Love,
> Bob"

THE FIRST
time is
the first
time. The
second
time think
again.

    •

There you
were,
all
the time.

    •

I can
not give
it back.

•

Your was there
here in any
way you
were.

Mazatlan: Sea

The sea flat out,
the light far out,
sky red, the
blobs of dark clouds
seem closer, beyond
the far lateral of
extended sea.

•

Shimmer of reflected
sand tones, the flat
ripples as the water
moves back—an oscil-
lation, endlessly in-
stinct movement—leaves
a ribbing after itself
it then returns to.

•

Bird flicker, light
sharp, flat—the
green hills of the two
islands make a familiar
measure, momently seen.

•

The air is thick
and wet and
comfortably encloses
with the sea's sounds.

•

Sleep—it washes
away.

KIDS WALKING beach,
minnow pools—
who knows which.

•

Nothing grand—
The scale is neither
big nor small.

•

Want to get the sense of "I" into Zukofsky's "eye"—a locus
of experience, not a presumption of expected value.

•

Here now—
begin!

B——

Crazy kid-face
skun, in water—
wide hips. The white,
white skin   a big
eared almost feral
toothed woman—
lovely in all particulars.

•

Other way—dark
eyed, the face a
glow of some other
experience, deepens
in the air.

AGH—MAN
thinks.

     •

Moving away in time,
as they say: *days
later*. Later than this—
what swings in the day's
particulars, one to one.

     •

An unexamined hump
at first of no
interest lifting out
of the beach at
last devoured us all.

     •

Sell the motherfucker for
several hundred dollars.

     •

". . . I ran out of my cabin, both glad and frightened, shouting, 'A noble earthquake! A noble earthquake!' feeling sure
I was going to learn something." [John Muir, *The Yosemite*,
p. 59.]

THE KICK
of the foot against . . .

     •

Make time
of irritations,
looking for the
recurrence—

waiting, waiting,
on the edge of its
to be there
where it was, waiting.

> .

Moving in the mind's
patterns, recognized
because there is where
they happen.

> .

Grease
on the hands—

Four

Before I die.
Before I die.
Before I die.
Before I die.

How THAT FACT of
seeing someone you love away
from you in time will
disappear in time, too.

> .

Here is all there is,
but *there* seems so
insistently across the way.

> .

Heal it, be
patient with
it—be quiet.

•

Across the
table,
years.

Here

Past time—those
memories opened
places and minds,
things of such reassurance—

now the twist,
and what was a road
turns to a circle
with nothing behind.

•

I didn't know what I could do.
I have never known it
but in doing found it
as best I could.

Here I am still,
waiting for that discovery.
What morning, what way now,
will be its token.

•

They all walk by
on the beach,
large, or little,
crippled, on the face
of the earth.

•

The wind holds
my leg like

a warm hand.

SOME NIGHTS, a fearful
waking—beside me
you were sleeping,
what your body was

a quiet, apparent
containment. All the world is
this tension, you or me,
seen in that mirror,

patent, pathetic, insured.
I grow bored with lives
of such orders—my own
the least if even yours the most.

·

No one lives in
the life of another—
no one knows.

In the singular
the many cohere,
but not to know it.

Here, *here*, the body
screaming its orders,
learns of its own.

·

What would you have
of the princess—
large ears, to hear?
Hands with soft fingers?

You will ride away
into the forest, you will
meet her there
but you will know her.

Why not another
not expected, some
lovely presence suddenly
declared?

All in your mind
the body is, and of
the body such
you make her.

·

One, two,
is the rule—

from there to three
simple enough.

Now four
makes the door

back again
to one and one.

·

My plan is
these little boxes
make sequences . . .

·

Lift me
from such I
makes such declaration.

·

Hearing it—*snivelling*—
wanting the reassurance of
another's decision.

There is no one precedes—
look ahead—and behind
you have only where you were.

You SEE the jerked
movement, in the
rigid frame, the
boy—the tense stricken

animal, and behind,
the sea moves and
relaxes. The island sits
in its immovable comfort.

What, in the head, goes wrong—
the circuit suddenly
charged with contraries,
and time only is left.

       •

The sun drops. The swimmers
grow black in the silver
glitter. The water slurs
and recurs. The air is soft.

COULD WRITE of fucking—
rather its instant or the slow
longing at times of its approach—

how the young man desires,
how, older, it is never known
but, familiar, comes to be so.

How your breasts, love,
fall in a rhythm also familiar,
neither tired nor so young they

push forward. I hate the metaphors.
I want you. I am still alone,
but want you with me.

Listless,
the heat rises—
the whole beach

vacant,
sluggish.
The forms shift

before we know,
before we thought
to know it.

The mind
again, the manner
of mind in the

body, the
weather, the waves,
the sun grows lower

in the faded
sky. Washed
out—the afternoon

of another day
with other people,
looking out of other eyes.

Only the
children, the sea,
the slight wind move

with the
same insistent
particularity.

•

I was sleeping
and saw the context
of people, dense
around me, talked
into their forms, almost

strident. There were
bright colors, intense
voices. We were, like
they say, discussing

some point of procedure—
would they go, or
come—and waking,
no one but my wife there,
the room faint, bare.

·

"It's strange. It's
all fallen
to grey."

·

How much
money is
there now?

Count it
again. There's
enough.

·

What changes.
Is the weather
all there is.

SUCH STRANGENESS of mind I know
I cannot find there more
than what I know.

I am tired of purposes,
intent that leads itself
back to its own belief. I want

nothing more of such brilliance
but what makes the shadows darker
and that fire grow dimmer.

•

Counting age as form
I feel the mark of one
who has been born and grown
to a little past return.

The body will not go
apart from itself to be
another possibility.
It lives where it finds home.

Thinking to alter all
I looked first to myself,
but have learned the foolishness
that wants an altered form.

Here now I am at best,
or what I think I am
must follow as the rest
and live the best it can.

•

There was no one there.
Rather I thought I saw her,
and named her beauty.

For that time we lived
all in my mind
with what time gives.

The substance of one
is not two. No thought
can ever come to that.

I could fashion another
were I to lose her.
Such is thought.

      •

Why the echo of
the old music
haunting all? Why

the lift and fall
of the old rhythms,
and aches and pains.

Why one, why two,
why not go utterly
away from all of it.

      •

Last night's dream of a complex of people, almost suburban
it seemed, with plots to uncover like a thriller. One moment
as we walk to some house through the dark, a man suddenly
appears behind us who throws himself at us, arms reaching
out, but falls short and lands, skids, spread-eagled on the
sidewalk. Then later, in another dream, we are bringing beer
somewhere on a sort of truck, rather the cab of one, nothing
back of it, and I am hanging on the side which I realize is
little more than a scaffolding—and the wheels nearly brush
me in turning. Then, much later, I hear our dog yelp—three
times it now seems—so vividly I'm awake and thinking he
must be outside the door of this room though he is literally in
another country. Reading Yeats: "May we not learn some day
to rewrite our histories, when they touch upon these things?"

WHEN HE and I,
after drinking and
talking, approached
the goddess or woman

become her, and by my
insistence entered
her, and in the ease
and delight of the

meeting I was given that
sight gave me myself,
this was the mystery
I had come to—all

manner of men, a
throng, and bodies of
women, writhing, and
a great though seemingly

silent sound—and when
I left the room to them,
I felt, as though hearing
laughter, my own heart lighten.

•

What do you do,
what do you say,
what do you think,
what do you know.

In London

"But what to do? and
What to do next?"

WILLIAM CARLOS WILLIAMS
A Voyage to Pagany

THAT DAY
in an oak tree—
fall's way
comes here.

•

Interrupt-
ions.

•

The room's spaces make the place
of the two persons' sitting seem
years across. One might accept
the "place" of one moving off as
in films a double image per-
mits that separation to be realized.

•

Fire the
half burnt
log, burning,
lies on.

•

Waked to past now dream
of previous place was about to
get all the confusions at last
resolved when he then woke up.

•

What is the
day of the
year we
sit in with
such fear.

WE'LL DIE
soon enough,
and be dead—

whence the whole
system
will fade from my head—

"but why the
tort-
ure . . ." as if

another circumstance
were forever
at hand.

·

Thinking of dying
à la Huxley on
acid so that
the beatific smile his
wife reported
was effect possibly
of the splendor of
all *possible* experience?

Or else, possibly,
the brain cells,
the whole organism,
exploding, im-
ploding, upon
itself, a galaxy
of light, energy,
forever more.

·

Die. Dead,
come alive.

Sign

What you know of me—
pale water.
The wind moves

that scattered cloud.
The shimmer of the air,
the sunlight

are perfect
in the mind,
the body.

PACING AS with some consequent
expectance, viz—"look out"—
the expected sequence then waited for.

    •

Come fly with me—like,
out of your mind is
no simile, no mere
description—what "mere,"
mare, *mère*, *mother*—
"here then," is what you want.

    •

Emily—simile.
What are you
staring at?

    •

I wanted to find something
worthy of respect—like
my family, any one one knows.

    •

What are you crossing all
those out for. A silence lasting
from then on . . .

•

Those out for.
From then on.

Round and round
all the corners.

Love—
let it

Out,
open up

Very,
very *voracious*ly—

Everywhere,
everyone.

Bobbie

"Every one
having the two."

Get it anyway
you can but first of all
eat it.

TIME TO GO
back where you
were going.

"DICKY THE Stick"—
a stick.

The Edge

Place it,
make the space

of it. Yellow,
that was a time.

He saw the stain of love
was upon the world,

a selvage, a faint
afteredge of color fading

at the edge of the world,
the edge beyond that edge.

You THINK in the circle
round the whole.

NOW THERE IS
still something.

Little Time —
and Place

You don't say
it is no
answer—you

don't say
it is no
answer.

•

After and after
round and around.

The so-called poet of love
is not so much silent as absorbed.
He ponders. He sits on
the hill looking over . . .

•

A day late—
your love was
still there.

•

Little bits
of it.

•

They are useful
people.

•

No sense one
should be different.

Dead in the year—
forms make friends.

"FINE CHINA.
A dollar twenty-nine."

IN THE
mouth—a
hand.

•

Hair is a
long thing
hanging
off.

•

Out the door

the
ass is

a
way.

•

Sitting—
shitting.

•

Fine manners,
weather,
cars and
people.

•

No air is
in this
room but
the sounds
occupy all
the space.

Rippling eyelids
with glister of moisture—

Long time no see.

The Teachings

of my grandmother
who at over eighty
went west from West Acton,
to see a long lost son named
Archie—by Greyhound, my
other uncle, Hap, got the *Globe*
to photograph her, and us—
came back from Riverside, California,
where Archie was—he'd left
at eighteen—and he'd tried,
she told us, to teach her
religion, "at her age"—"as
much a fool as ever"—and
she never spoke of him again.

Dreary, heavy
accumulation
of guilts, debts—
all in the head.

        •

A wind I can
hear outside shifts
the mind, day, eye's
center. A kind.

Kiki

World in a
plastic octa-
gon from a
most perspica-
cious daughter.

A Wall

for Tom

Afternoon lengthens like sunlight
also shrinking as the day comes
to its end in the flickering light.

The leaves make it like that,
the wind moves them, the trees
tower so high above the room's space.

I had walked into a wall, not
through but against it, felt my
shoulder hit its literal hardness.

Sunday. Nothing to worship but
myself, my own body and those
related—my wife, my children, my friends—

but outside, light, it grows long,
lengthens. This world of such changes,
nothing stable but in that motion.

Oh spaces. Dance. Make happiness.
Make the simple the changing—
a little ode to much hopefulness.

ALL AROUND
the town
he walked.

THE MEN in my life were
three in number, a
father, uncle, grand-

father—and with that
father an interchangeable
other—the *Man*—whom

to score with, scream at.
The *wind* rises in a
fucking, endless volume.

NEITHER SADNESS nor desire
seems the edge: this precipice.

DELIGHT DANCES,
everything works.

How WISE age is—
how desirous!

LOVE'S FAINT trace . . .

THE SMELL of stale air
in this cramped room.
One sits. The shit falls
below the seat into water.

You HAVE nor face nor hands
nor eyes nor head either.

In London

for Bettina

Homage to Bly & Lorca
_____

"I'm going home to Boston
by God"

    •

Signs
_____

(red)

EXIT
EXIT
EXIT
EXIT

    •

(Cards)

Question—
where do you get a pencil.
Answer.

_____

    •

(for Jim Dine)

most common simple
address words everything
in one clear call to me.

    •

("Small Dreams")

Scaffolding comes up the side of the building, pipes, men
putting them there. Faces, in, past one block of windows,

then as I'm up in the bathroom, they appear there too.

•

Ted
is ready.
The bell
rings.

•

Small dreams of home.
Small of home dreams.
Dreams of small home.
Home small dreams of.

•

I love you happily
ever after.

•

(Homesick, etc.)

There is a land
far, far away
and I will go there
every day.

•

12:30 (Read as Twelve Thirty)

(Berrigan
Sleeps on)

•

Voices on the phone, over it—wires? Pulsations. Lovely one
of young woman. Very soft and pleasant. Thinking of Chamberlain and Ultra Violet—"talking the night away." Fuck
MacCluhan—or how the hell you spell it—and/or teetering
fall, the teething ring, "The Mother of Us All"—*for Bob*. Call
me up. "Don't Bring Me Down . . ."

•

Variance of emotional occasion in English voices—for myself, American, etc. Therefore awkward at times "to know

where one is." In contrast to Val's Welsh accent—the congruence with one's own, Massachusetts. Not that they "sound alike"—but somehow do agree.

•

"London
Postal Area
A-D"

•

Posterior possibilities—
Fuck 'em.

•

"It's 2 hrs. 19 mins. from London
in the train to beautiful country."

"EAT ME"
The favorite delicious dates.

•

Girls
Girls
Girls
Girls

2 X 2

•

Some guy now here inside wandering around with ladder and bucket. Meanwhile the scaffolding being built outside goes on and on, more secure.

•

Like German's poem I once translated, something about "when I kissed you, a beam came through the room. When I picked you flowers, they took the whole house away." Sort of an ultimate hard-luck story.

•

Lovely roofs outside.
Some of the best roofs in London.

•

Surrounded
by bad art.

.

I get
a lot
of writing
done—

"You Americans."

.

H—will pirate primary edition of Wms' *Spring and All*, i.e.,
it's all there. Check for Whitman's *An American Primer*—long
time out of print. Wish he'd reprint as Chas apparently sug-
gests Gorki's *Reminiscences of Tolstoi* [now learn it's been in
paperback for some years]. Wish I were home at this precise
moment—the sun coming in those windows. The sounds
of the house, birds too. Wish I were in bed with Bobbie, just
waking up.

.

Wish I were an apple seed
and had John what's-his-name
to plant me.

.

Her strict eye,
her lovely voice.

.

Così fan tutte.
So machin's alle.

.

Wigmore
dry gin
kid.

.

Wish Joan Baez was here
singing "Tears of Rage" in my ear.

Wish I was Bob Dylan—
he's got a subtle mind.

    •

I keep coming—
I keep combing my hair.

    •

Peter Grimes
Disraeli Gears

    •

That tidy habit of sound
relations—must be in the
very works,* like.

---

*Words work
the author of many pieces

    •

Wish could snap pix in
mind forever of roofs out
window. Print on endurable paper, etc.

    •

With delight he realized
his shirts would last him.

    •

I'll get home in 'em.

    •

The song of such energy
invites me. The song

of

THERE IS a space
of trees—

long since, all
there—

So Big

The night's eye
he could say
blandly.

A
word goes
forward—

hands down. She
sleeps beside
him, is

elsewhere. The
movie goes on,
the people

hurt each other.
Now say to her,
love is all.

Sweet, sad
nostalgia—
walking

by on the
beach a
kid in two

piece bathing
suit of awful
color, girl

with small
breasts, furtive,
half-terrified

a man who
might have been
screaming, a

woman, more
lush, huge, somewhat
fallen

breasts. Waves
coming in as
the tide

goes out, either York Beach,
Maine,
1937 or else

waking, kicking at
the water, the
sand between my toes.

     •

Let me see what you're looking at,
behind you, up close, my head pressed

against you, let me look at what
it is you are seeing, all by yourself.

     •

Echoes—what
air trembles to
sound out like
waves one watches.

I DON'T HATE you lately,
nor do I think to
hate you

lately. Nor then nor now—
lately—no
hate—for me,

for you.

Way

The walls constituting our
access to the property—

then the path through it,
the walls of that access.

LOOKING FOR a way
the feet find it.

If mistaken, the
hands were not.

Ears hear. Eyes
see everything.

The mind only
takes its time.

BLESSÉD WATER, blesséd man . . .
How long to find you,
how long looking at what is inevitable?

Soup

for Mike and Joanna

Trembling
with delight—
mind takes forms

from faces,
finds
happiness

delicious . . .

PEOPLE WITHOUT their own scene
lean.

Two Times

Image
docteur

ee-maj
dok-turr

That's a beautiful coat.

"YOUR WISH came true
to my surprise."

I WANT TO fuck you
from two to four

endlessly
the possibility

I want to
fuck you

•

Charmed
by his own reward.

•

A trembling now
throughout.

•

I am here.

Thinking

Had not
thought
of it . . .

    •

Had nor thought
nor vacancy—

a space
between. Linkage:

the system, the
one after another—

Though the words
agree? Though

the sounds
sound. The sea,

the woods, *those*
echoing hills . . .

    •

Even in a wood
they stood—

even without sound
they are around.

Here and there, and
everywhere.

    •

All you people
know everything!

All you know you know.
Hence nothing else to?

—Laugh at
that dichotomy.

E.g., the one again
from another one.

Hold it—
to unfold it open.

.

He wants to sit down
on a chair

he holds in the air
by putting it there.

He wants to sleep in a bed
he keeps in his head.

THE DAY was gathered on waking
into a misty greyness. All the air
was muffled with it, the colors
faded. Not simply then alone—

the house despite its size is full
with us—but an insistent restless
sense of nowhere enough to be
despite the family, the fact of us.

What does one want—more, what
do I say I want. Words give
me sense of something. Days I find
had use for me, how else one thought.

But the nagging, the dripping
weather . . . All the accumulation,
boxes of things piled up the grey
seems to cover, all the insistent junk.

One comes to a place he had not thought to,
looks ahead to whatever,
feels nothing lost but himself.

Look

Doesn't he *see*
in the tree
something of *me?*

Or there
wears
no clothes

at all. He
wants
to go

home, *home*—
he wants
to go home.

I WAS NEVER SO upset
as when last I met

another idiot walking by
with much the same preoccupations as I.

FALLING DOWNHILL—
A ball
That falls
And so
Keeps up with itself.

The Message

He was wise,
they said,

in being dead.
Nothing more could be said—

But that incredible
idealism, the blur
of the language, how
it says nothing.

Nothing more than that
will do, all
people are
susceptible after all.

Fall

Again you
feel the air
be light a
smoke would
burn in.

Leaves, leaves,
the hill we
drive up over-
hung with leaves,
the trees all covered.

IT IS FUNNY—strange—to see the young
swirl—leaves, they might be
said to be, in a current of our own.

The limp gestures of older persons,
the hands unable to hold them, all
the world in a flaccid attentiveness—

Now it is fall, and one must yield
again to the end of a cycle, call
it *spring*, and its endless instances.

You will never be here
again, you will never

see again what you now see—
you, the euphemistic

I speaks always, always
wanting a you to be *here*.

•

How the I
speaks to
you—
over hills.

Continuing forward with a trembling
slipshod insistent sense of affection—
the privileges of vacations, the houses
they have stayed in, the past,

the present, the faces he sees
sometimes before him, the all-
too-suspended times something
less pleasant has proved the case—

his mother's, his sister's, face,
his hands, the outsized now
lower part of his left thumb
from an accident, in Gloucester, last summer—

"Where are all the swallows gone . . ."
as if it were a song he wanted
to remember, had written down to
place among the other things along

a road in summer, such nostalgia,
such airs the summer wears. The grasses
blow and to and fro must walk
all the *things* of life about which one talked.

Persons

for Charles

That this wondering two-footed
notion of abeyance should
think to move and have
come to her and to him
a *nature* and a *place*.

      •

Throw out the *water*—let the land
sit up on it—or in it—
be the wake which forms
at the back of the boat from
all the odds and ends of things.

      •

Name the name again, play that
song again. Let the woods roar
in echo again. There is *sun*
as quality of *up* as well as
light fades in the evening, always.

Dying

If we are to exist,
a *we* of an imagination of
more than one, a

veritable multiplicity!
What a day
it is—what

one of many
days and many people,
who live here.

You may bring it
in now
to me. That,

one says, is
the multiplicity—
dying.

"Do You Think . . ."

Do you think that if
you once do what you want
to do you will want not to do it.

Do you think that if
there's an apple on the table
and somebody eats it, it
won't be there anymore.

Do you think that if
two people are in love with one another,
one or the other has got to be
less in love than the other at
some point in the otherwise happy relationship.

Do you think that if
you once take a breath, you're by
that committed to taking the next one
and so on until the very process of
breathing's an endlessly expanding need
almost of its own necessity forever.

Do you think that if
no one knows then whatever
it is, no one will know and
that will be the case, like
they say, for an indefinite
period of time if such time
can have a qualification of such time.

Do you know anyone,
really. Have you been, really,
much alone. Are you lonely,

now, for example. Does anything
really matter to you, really, or
has anything mattered. Does each
thing tend to be there, and then not
to be there, just as if that were it.

Do you think that if
I said, *I love you*, or anyone
said it, or you did. Do you
think that if you had all
such decisions to make and could
make them. Do you think that
if you did. That you really
would have to think it all into
reality, that world, each time, new.

Mary's Fancy

The world pours in
on wings of song.
The radio says
whatever told to

but in mind, air
of another kind,
it holds a place
in the air's space.

Sounds now are
so various, a pig,
goat's bleat. The
burros somewhere.

The air hums, tick
of a watch, motor's
blur outside, a sequent
birds' tweeting. All

the ambient movement
neither seen nor
felt but endlessly,
endlessly heard.

Two

Holding
for one
instant this
moment—

•

In mind, in
other places.

THE WALL
one's up against,
the flesh turned stone—

Mind's eye
was memory's
as well as all

those things
that happened. The days
passing, sun

rose and set.
The mind
delighted, else

was tired
of all the flutter
and grew quiet.

The body sometimes
followed,
sometimes led.

There is
or was
no separation

ever, save only
in the head
that knows all.

QUICK TALK
their speech—

will mother
live longer,

will anything
be again here

whatever
it was?

A Testament

1

We resolve to think of ourselves,
insofar as one of us can so speak

of the other, as involved with
a necessary system, of age and its

factors. We will not be otherwise
than what we are. Our skin

growing more wrinkled, our hair
grey, will not be other than that.

We will laugh, smile, on provocation.
No hysterics shall obtain. We will

love perhaps in other modes but the
yearning, at least my own, will not

grow less, and as I sit now writing this,
a sense of time passing surely,

but with nothing of itself to say,
opaque as the night, dense, always there.

2

Not being dumb
I won't be nor you

either, I think. Not
resistance but no

less than everything,
a rage to keep

even in all respects.
The crickets' humming,

the longer intervals
of other insect

sounds, the birds,
tree toads—al-

ready the ear
has come to hear,

won't accept less.
Say that *I* is

the accumulation
of *my* virtues—breath

lasts, some simile
of water

slopping
to and fro.

3

When they
come to get me,
I'll

give them
you instead—
ashamed,

even trembling
in that fear
of love's

insistences.
But its generosity
will know

I don't go
easily
dragging you after.

Harry

You're sucking
for a bruise
we used to say.

THE DEATH of
one is
none.

The death of
one is
many.

The Act of Love

for Bobbie

Whatever constitutes
the act of love,
save physical

encounter, you are
dear to me,
not value as

with banks—
but a meaning self-
sufficient, dry

at times as sand,
or else the trees,
dripping with

rain. How shall
one, this so-
called person,

say it? He
loves, his mind
is occupied, his

hands move
writing words
which come

into his head.
Now here,
the day surrounds

this man
and woman
sitting a small

distance apart.
Love will not
solve it—but

draws closer,
always, makes
the moisture of their

mouths and bodies
actively
engage. If I

wanted
a dirty picture,
would it always

be of a
woman straddled?
Yes

and no, these
are true opposites,
a you and me

of non-
sense,
for our love.

Now, one
says, the wind
lifts, the sky

is very blue, the
water just
beyond me makes

its lovely sounds.
How *dear*
you are

to me, how love-
ly all your
body *is*, how

all these
senses do
commingle, so

that in your very
arms I still
can think of you.

Time

Moment to
moment the
body seems

to me to
be there: a
catch of

air, pattern
of space— Let's
walk today

all the way
to the beach,
let's think

of where we'll be
in two years'
time, of where

we *were*. Let
the days go.
Each moment is

of such paradoxical
definition—a
waterfall that would

flow backward
if it could. It
can? My time,

one thinks,
is drawing to
some close. This

feeling comes
and goes. No
measure ever serves

enough, enough—
so "finish it"
gets done, alone.

The Problem

He can say, I am
watching a boat tug
at its mooring, a small

rowboat. It is almost
three in the
afternoon. Myself

and my wife are
sitting on the porch
of a house in Grand-

Case, Saint Martin,
French West Indies—
and he says it.

The Tiger

Today we saw a tiger
with two heads come
bounding out of the

forest by the corner of
Main and Bailey. We
were not afraid. The

war had stopped fifteen
minutes previous, we
had stopped in a bar

to celebrate, but now
stood, transfixed,
by another fear.

The Birds

for Jane and Stan Brakhage

I'll miss the small birds that come
for the sugar you put out
and the bread crumbs. They've

made the edge of the sea domestic
and, as I am, I welcome that.
Nights my head seemed twisted

with dreams and the sea wash,
I let it all come quiet, waking,
counting familiar thoughts and objects.

Here to rest, like they say, I best
liked walking along the beach
past the town till one reached

the other one, around the corner
of rock and small trees. It was
clear, and often empty, and

peaceful. Those lovely ungainly
pelicans fished there, dropping
like rocks, with grace, from the air,

headfirst, then sat on the water,
letting the pouch of their beaks
grow thin again, then swallowing

whatever they'd caught. The birds,
no matter they're not of our kind,
seem most like us here. I want

to go where they go, in a way, if
a small and common one. I want
to ride that air which makes the sea

seem down there, not the element
in which one thrashes to come up.
I love water, I *love* water—

but I also love air, and fire.

On Vacation

Things seem empty
on vacation if the labors
have not been physical,

if tedium was rather
a daily knot, a continuum,
if satisfaction was almost

placid. On Sundays the restlessness
grows, on weekends, on
months of vacation myself grows

vacuous. Taking walks, swimming,
drinking, I am always afraid
of having more. Hence a true

Puritan, I shall never rest from my labors
until all rest with me, until I am
driven by that density home.

Sounds

Some awful
grating sound
as if some monstrous
nose were being blown.

      •

Yuketeh, *yuketeh*—
moves slow through the water.

      •

Velvet purr,
resting—

      •

Slosh, slush,
longer wash
of it. Con-
verses.

      •

Tseet, *tseet*—
then chatter,
all the way home.

Moment

Whether to *use* time, or to *kill* time, either
still preys on my mind.

One's come now to the graveyard,
where the bones of the dead are.

All roads *have* come
here, truly common—

except the body is moved,
still, to some other use.

An Illness

The senses of one's
life begin
to fade. Rather,

I ask, who is the man
who feels he
thinks he knows.

I had felt
the way accumulated,
coming from that past,

a prospect beckoned, like
the lovely
nineteenth century. Women

one grew up to
then were there.
Even the smallest

illness changes
that. I saw you
stop, a moment.

The hospital
was a pitiful
construct and

a scaffolding upset
all dignity of
entrance, somehow.

But now it's rather
the people I sat with
yesterday. Across from me

a young woman, dark
haired, and in
her eyes much dis-

traction, and fear. The
other one I
remember was also

young, a man, with
lovely eyes, a greyish
blue. He was

struck by what
we were
hearing, a voice,

on a tape, of an
old friend, recently dead.
Have you noticed

the prevalence
of grey blue eyes?
Is it

silly, somehow,
so to see them?
Your breasts

grow softer now
upon their
curious stem. In

bed I yearn
for softness, turning
always to you. Don't,

one wants to cry,
desert me! Have I
studied

all such isolation
just to
be alone?

Robinson Crusoe
is a
favorite book. I thought

it was a true one.
Now I find
I wonder. Now

it changes. Do you
know that line
that speaks of music

fading up a woodland
path? Or is it
a pasture

I have in mind?
I remember pastures
of my childhood but

I will not
bore you with their
boulders and cows.

Rather those smells,
and flowers—
the lady slippers,

all the quiet darkness
of the woods. Where
have I come to,

who is here. What
a sad cry
that seems, and I

reject it. On
and on. And many,
many years, one

thinks, remain.
Tremulous, we
waver, here. We

love all
worlds we
live in.

People

for Arthur Okamura

I knew where they were,
in the woods. My sister
made them little houses.

Possibly she was one,
or had been one
before. They were there,

very small but quick,
if I moved. I
never saw them.

How big is small. What
are we in. Do
these forms of us take shape, then.

Stan told us of the shape
a march makes, in
anger, a sort of small

head, the vanguard, then
a thin neck, and then,
following out, a kind of billowing,

loosely gathered *body*, always
the same. It must be
people seen from above

have forms, take place,
make an insistent pattern,
not suburbs, but the way

they gather in public places,
or, hidden from others,
look one by one, must be

there to see, a record if
nothing more. "In a tree
one may observe the hierarchies

of monkeys," someone says. "On
the higher branches, etc." But
not like that, no, the kids

run, watch the *wave* of them
pass. See the form of their
movement pass, like the wind's.

I love you, I thought,
suddenly. My hands
are talking again. In-

side each finger must
be several men. They
want to talk to me.

On the floor the dog's eye
reflects the world, the people
passing there, before him.

The car holds possibly
six people, comfortably,
though each is many more.

I'll never die or else will
be the myriad people all
were always and must be—

in a flower, in a
hand, in some
passing wind.

　　　•

These things
seen from inside, human,
a head, hands

and feet. I can't
begin again to make
more than was made.

You'll see them
as flowers, called
the flower people—

others as rocks,
or silt, some
crystalline or even

a stream of smoke.
Why here at all
—the first question—

no one easily answers,
but they've taken place
over all else. They live

now in everything, as everything.
I keep hearing
their voices, most happily

laughing, but the screaming
is there also. Watch
how they go together.

They are not isolated
but meld into continuous
place, one to one, never alone.

•

From whatever place
they may have come from,
from under rocks,

that moistness, or the sea,
or else in those
slanting places of darkness,

in the woods, they
are here and ourselves
with them. All

the forms we know,
the designs, the
closed-eye visions of

order—these too they are,
in the skin we
share with them.

If you twist one
even insignificant part
of your body

to another, imagined
situation of where it
might be, you'll

feel the pain of all
such distortion and
the voices will

flood your head with
terror. No thing
you can do can

be otherwise than
these *people*, large
or small, however

you choose to think
them—a drop of
water, glistening

on a grassblade, or
the whole continent,
the whole world of *size*.

•

Some stories begin,
when I was young—
this also. It tells

a truth of things,
of people. There used
to be so many, so

big one's eyes went
up them, like a ladder,
crouched in a wall.

Now grown large, I
sometimes stumble, walk
with no knowledge of

what's under foot.

  •

Some small
echo
at the earth's edge

recalls
these voices,
these small

persistent
movements,
these people,

the circles,
the holes they
made, the

one
multiphasic
direction,

the going,
the coming,
the lives.

I
fails in
the forms

of them, I
want
to go home.

Christmas: May 10, 1970

Flicker
of *this* light
on consciousness—a

light,
light, green
light, green

tree is the
life. Christmas,
for Christ's

sake, god
damn all thieves!
Green, *green*—

light, goes
by in a
flash.

Massachusetts

What gentle echoes,
half heard sounds
there are around here.

　　·

You place yourself in
such relation, you hear
everything that's said.

Take it or leave it.
Return it to a particular
condition.

Think
slowly. See
the things around you,

taking place.

•

I began wanting a sense
of melody, e.g., following
the tune, became somehow
an image, then several,
and I was watching those things
becoming in front of me.

•

The *you* imagined locates
the response. Like turning
a tv dial. The message,
as one says, is information,
a form of energy. The wisdom
of the ages is "electrical" impulse.

•

Lap of water
to the hand, lifting
up, slaps
the side of the dock—

Darkening air, heavy
feeling in the air.

•

A PLAN

On some summer day
when we are far away
and there is impulse and time,
we will talk about all this.

Somebody Died

What shall we know we don't know,
that we know we know we don't know.

•

The head walks
down the
street with
an umbrella.

•

People
were walking
by.

•

They will think of anything
next, the woman says.

June 6, 1970

We will write a
simple epic of
sly lust, all

the things we
think of will
be there. He,

says, *sand*, she,
a large cup
of something, someone

screams, all over,
the world erupts,
people laugh.

For Benny and Sabina

So lovely, now, the day
quiets. What one hoped
for is realized. All

one's life has
come to this, all
is here. And it

continues taking place
for a long time.
The day recovers

itself, air feels
a wet, heavy quiet.
Grey, if one could see the sky.

I felt around myself
for something. I could
almost see you in wanting you there.

It's a hard life at times,
thoughtful, very careful
of all it seems to find.

For Betsy and Tom

We are again
walking in a
straight line—feet

fall, footsteps. We
walk! I am
happy, foolish I

stumble on to the next
person, I think
to myself, charming in

the peace she so manifestly
carries with her. All the
children follow us. The

dogs walk also,
with a sort of sedateness.
They think

they think. We
whistle. I want to
love everyone alive!

Song

You look out and you see people.
You have some reason in mind.
You are there in a real sense.

I used to
think of the
reasons as if I

knew them. My name
is Bob, I'm
friendly. You can't

go home now. This
is a song,
so they say.

For Allen

Air of heaven sings.
Raspberries ripen. *Air*
is a familiar presence.

See the dog walk
across the street. He
is limping because you are looking.

Irish

Her cunt lifts on a
velvet couch, red
velvet, the cry of

Ireland. All the people
I've ever known
salute her. My dear

woman, why have you
left here, why are
you unhappy?

SITTING UP to fill pages having written the poem following
"ahead." Allen's sense so echoes for me—those "mind trips"
he gives me the fact and responsibility of. I really at times
have no idea of what would be "right conduct." Reading this
afternoon about 100 pages of his "Indian Journals"—what
difference—such detail—such a specific personal *head*—
isn't that mind? Last night the lady, lovely, vigorous, at the
"Dunkin Donuts" no less, who gives me the 2 dozen now to
be stale ones—"abstract"? I think the *act* can never be.
We're all, in our sense of it, fugitives, all "on the way"—*if* we
think at all. Tom, Betsy, Kirsten, Darrell, David, Eliza-
beth—Sarah and Kate—and Spot—and Tiger Sam with his
toe now given to eternity. *We'll* get there.

You

Back and forth across
time, lots of things
one needs one's

hand held for. Don't
stumble, in the dark. Keep
walking. This is life.

Walking the Dog

The one to one
walking talk
of the dog—the line

of the dog, tail,
hair
of the dog—

trying,
in reality,
to walk:

a *description*,—hey!
see the dog
walk—a

memory of some
poor son of a bitch dog
walking. Walk

all the way, you'll
get there, poor,
poor dog.

Envoi

Particulars they want,
particulars they
fucking well will

get, love. For openers,
you—the stars
earth revolves about,

the galaxies their in-
struments neglect. I
walk down a road

you make ahead, not
(no negative) there ex-
cept my body finds

it. Love, love,
love, swirls—myriad
insects hum, the

air softens, the night
is *here*. So empty
these days with-

out you, a box
with nothing in it. I
am waiting, you

are coming, so what's
the world but
all of it.

Heaven

"I don't want
my tits
particularized"—

five men in
yellow costumes sneak
into the wings.

I know what's
going on in that
biological waiting room.

Peace, brother,
and sister, and
mother, and you guys.

Peace

Waiting for a bus,
the bus, vehicle gets me
home to something
where dinner

is prepared with care,
love is found in the icebox,
the bed made, the
clock strikes eleven.

Oh love, oh rocks,
of time, oh ashes I
left in the bucket,—
care, care, care, care.

Wisdom

You could go on
talking to an imaginary
person, real flesh
and blood likewise—

and be none the wiser.
Truth is a small
stream one steps over,
wisdom an insistent preoccupation.

Echo

I'm almost
done, the hour
echoes, what

are those words
I heard, was
it *flower*, *stream*,

Nashe's, as Allen's
saying it, "Brightness
falls from the air"?

Was I never here?
The hour, the day
I lived some

sense of it?
All wrong? What
was it then

got done? This
life a stepping
up or down

some progress?
Here, *here*,
the only form

I've known.

Trees

Thighs, *trees*—
you want
a place to stand,
stand on it.

Body, a vacant
hole, winds blow
through it—the
resonance, of experience,

all words are a vi-
bration, head, chest,
trunk, of tree, has
limbs, grows leaves.

Person

Gee, I know
a lovely girl,
woman she
calls herself—did

you ever see a
human being plain,
the body so
inclined? Let me

introduce to
myself myself. I am
one of the race.
I speak an English.

For Anybody

I could climb a mountain
for a view.

     •

If you get sillier
as you get older,
as you get younger,
that's really abstract.

     •

Allen's got me
on the ropes. I
think of them
all around me.

He went around
the world to see it
and it is as he'd say
there to see.

We're friends, blood
for blood. Death if you want,
we'll pay those dues.
I wouldn't assume

his responsibility
in anything I'd say or do
except I love him
and read what he writes.

     •

I'm really writing
a valentine in
summer, such
a lovely season.

Here in New England
at last, *at last*—
where I was born,
now they tell me.

For Chuck ◇ Hinman

So big
the *out there:*
if the one
moves, a pink
faint light, *cut*
each of the
four the *same*, they
are the same:
all around.

For Lewis, to Say It

All one knows, and knows
upon the possibility of knowing,
knowing some-

thing, a thing
that, driven, in-
sists upon its

knowledge. The
ice *melts*, the
water re-

forms, as in a
jail, persons
are *corrected*. I

will not
not succeed. That world
to me is *not* possible.

"Oh, Love . . ."

Oh love, falling—
the words one
tries

to say are
facts, the
steps, the

walk down
place
and time.

On Acid

And had no actual
hesitancies, always
(flickering) mind's
sensations: here, here, *here**

philo-tro-

bic-port-

a-bil-ity?

End, end, end, end, end, end

Next? Next who/ who/ they we

                    for she me

_____
*or there?   is not we'll

                be . . . . .

Pay

Walking down a
walk, a stone
sees, *assizes*, sizes,

taxes, form
forms. It
says, it is

here—dull,
the de-
scription, it

never seizes,
ever says
enough.

"For Some Weeks . . ."

for Kirsten

For some weeks
now, caught in my
own complexities, I'd

been thinking
of you, first as
to have your

first child, then
(since not to) as
a woman now

entirely. My
own life, I
thought, this curious

space suit one
lives in, becomes
insistent also.

Think
of Andean flutes
filling the room

with mountains no less!
Dancing, you can
see the goats above you.

Or is it water,
as ever, one feels the
flooding of?

"Liquid notes"—
passion so articulately
carefree, at last.

I've been eating
too much. At times
I feel my stomach

will burst into the room.
My eye seems
to blur at close print.

Pieces
fall away dis-
closing another place.

These faces,
younger, a letter
from someone unknown,

collect much as
whatever would
falling off.

My mother comes
to visit soon. This
part of the country,

New England,
is most her home—
in ways not mine.

I remember
sitting in my sister's
dining-room in Berkeley

with you both
either side—a
warm and open

sunlit day. Possibly
we'll both wander
a long way.

When you first
left home, I had
fears—now

pride fills me,
a man with
a daughter a woman.

Happiness to you,
bless the world
you're given.

Hunger

He knows
the hunger, walking
in that stiff-legged fashion.

She
knows the hunger,
all her body keeps

telling you you
are not
her. It is

here, I saw
it here. Where
are the people.

Try to
shut me up,
I said, keep

pushing you'll
get it, he,
or someone, said.

I have been,
I *was*, I
am, also.

Jesus Christ, another
one we
got to put up with—

people, and
people, and people,
and people—trees

on Michigan Ave—as
photographed by Harry
Callahan—*trees*,

"I think
that I
will never

see—"
I want some-
thing to eat and

trees—drink
water, places, a
tree in

the hole. We have
to leave

now.

Rain

Things one sees through
a blurred sheet of glass,
that figures, predestined,
conditions of thought.

·

Things seen through
plastic, rain sheets,
trees blowing in a blurred
steady sheet of vision.

·

Raining, trees blow,
limbs flutter, leaves
wet with the insistent
rain, all over, everywhere.

·

Harry will write
Mabel on Monday.
The communication
of human desires

flows in an apparently
clear pattern, aftersight,
now they know
for sure what it was.

If it rains, the woods
will not be so dry
and danger averted,
sleep invited.

Rain (2)

Thoughtful of you, I was
anticipating change in
the usual manner. If the rain

made the day unexpected,
in it I took a place.
But the edge of the room

now blurred, or the window
did, or you, sitting, had
nonetheless moved away.

Why is it an empty house
one moves through, shouting
these names of people there?

Down Home

Water
neither knows
who drinks
it nor
denies.

.

Come
to the
fair
was true
invitation.

.

Who has
less in there
being *more*?

.

I, I, I,
chatter.

.

The kid
outside the house
walking.

.

Is hunger
only automatic
appetite?

.

Answers:
all
right.

.

Quick
idea of
here was
the place.

.

Never
again
here.

For Marisol

A little
water
falls.

Night

Needs most
happily mutual,
this given,
that taken,

the board clear,
and the food
reappears as
one after one

the night finds
persons in a
lovely particular
display. Here

is a street, and
now a car seems
to be coming,
the lights

signal approach at
an intersection when
a locked group
beats upon the

locked door an
inextricable tenderness
of one man's
desire to be there.

Mouths Nuzz

Mouths nuzz-
ling, "seeking
in blind
love," mouths nuzz-

ling, "seek-
ing in
blind
love . . ."

Kid

The kid left
out back waits
for his mother's

face to
reappear
in

a win-
dow,
waving.

A Tiny Place

Walking down
backward, wall
fall, waters

talk, a
crash, much
sound of

noise, *pa-*
tience, a
tiny place.

     •

(Takes
place)

Smoke

Again in space,
elsewhere,
displaced as they say,

an envoi
to you, thinking
of you, delaying

direct thought perhaps,
since you aren't
here, weren't more

than substantial the
last sight
of you—why

shouldn't there be
the possibility of many lives,
all lived

as one. I don't know,
I don't, can't,
believe it, want

you there,
here, *be*
with me.

Smoke
comes of burning, lifts
in the air that signal,

fades
away, blown,
taken.

Knokke

for Bobbie

Did you notice all the water
in front of you, and the Magrittes,
both murals and what must be

their initial instance, in that room,
at the Casino, where I guess
I'll speak? Funny, walking,

talking to you, passing these
stubby, curious people, the little
bathhouses, some on cart wheels,

labeled "CÉLINE," "FILIP,"
and so on, seeing as I walk
back here, alone, such a distance

to the west, sun shine on waves,
the wind against me, and fall
already here now. You aren't here,

you may never be
as I've known you
again. It's a long way.

Knokke, Belgium, 5:55 P.M., in
room of Hotel Simoens, 9/4/70

Echoes

A sudden
loss of hope,
flutters, the
loss of something
known too well.

Roads

It may be grubs
and worms and
simple change

make the conversion.
I don't think
anymore with clarity,

myself reportedly,
and known as well,
the center of it,

uglinesses, swarms
of discontent, lack-
lustre feeling in

the days. Nights one
doesn't think of, tries
to feel again

what was the way
which brought us here?
To have come to it alone?

Love

Tracking through this
interminable sadness—

like somebody said,
change the record.

Mobile Homes

Driving along the coast road
with people picked up in passing,

a Roman elegance describes—
often stoned and with an ease

of a car's working well and
silent companions—

describes what fixtures are,
those destinations, places one

means to come to, detrituses,
decisions, mobile homes.

Curse

The one

man who will
not fuck me
tonight will

be you.

Epigraph

Lot's wife,
married to chance,
luck's, fortune's
foolish bride.

"Bolinas and Me . . ."

for Stan Persky

Bolinas and me.
Believe me.

Roy Kiyooka
not here

says that.
Say this.

The human,
the yearning,

human situation
wanting something to be,

which is.
What's wanted?

Let the man put the gas in
your car, John, e.g.,

complete doing what
you wanted him to.

Have *done* with it?
Ham on rye.

The sea, the drive
along the coast in L.A.

I remember Joanne. I
want to. She's

lovely, one says.
So she is. So

are you too.
Or one. Have

done with it.
You see that

line of rocks out there?
Water, waves, two

dead sea lions,
says Peter. He's

lovely. All of them.
Let's walk down

to the beach, see
the sea, say.

If you love someone,
you'd better believe it,

and/or you could,
could write

that all night,
all right. All wrong.

All—isn't enough.
I want to get going. Here's love.

Drive home, up through the mountains,
dense fog. See the car lights

make way of it. See
the night, all around.

Bleed, into the toilet,
two nights, two days,

away from whatever,
go home, and stay there?

I want to walk around here,
look at the people, pretty,

look at the houses, stop in
the bar, get the mail, get

going again, somewhere.
One, two, three, four.

Husbands and fathers.
Sweet love, sweet love.

The kids come
by on bicycles, the little,

increasingly large
people, in the rain.

The liquor store lights
shine out in the night,

and one is walking, going,
coming, in the night.

Holy place we stand in,
these changes—Thanksgiving,

in the circle of oaks,
the sun going west, a glowing

white yellow through the woods.
To the west all the distance.

Things move. You've come to here
by one thing after another, and are here.

Flat thoughts in recalling
something after. Nostalgic twist

of everything so thought—a
period of thought here.

Hair falling, black tangle,
standing in front of the fire,

love dancing, silent, a figure,
a feeling, felt and moving here.

After all it speaks
less in saying more. It, it—

the hunk of wood is
not burning.

Marriage burns, soars—
all day the roar of it

from the lovely barnspace.
The people, the plenitude of all

in the open clearing, the sunlight, lovely densities. I am

slowly going, coming home. *Let
go, let go of it.* Walking

and walking, dream of those
voices, people again, not

quite audible though I can
see them, colors, forms,

a chatter just back of the ear,
moving toward them, the edge

of the woods. Again and
again and again, how

insistent, this blood one
thinks of as in

the body, these hands,
this face. Bolinas sits on the ground

by the sea, sky
overhead.

Sea

Salt and water,
beach sloped form,
wind and water,
it all comes home.

See days
forward, weeks
on end,
opened again.

Past, west,
backwards
water's wake,
a lot of boats.

Billfold

Piece of me, curiously
attached, you were in

a bar for two days un-
drinking and unthinking,
object of your own worth.

For the Graduation
Bolinas School, June 11, 1971

for Sarah

Pretension has it
you can't
get back
what's gone by.

Yet I don't believe it.
The sky
in this place
stays here

and the sun
comes, or goes
and comes again,
on the same day.

We live in a circle,
older or younger,
we go round
and around on this earth.

I was trying to remember
what it
was like
at your age.

His Idea

LET SOMETHING else be
the question—
while I fuck again:

an instruction to youth,
and age,
with its various occasion.

This time you will
be so substantial
I will go to sleep.

INSISTENT
this yearning
toward
union,
states,
bodies,
dogs.

FANTASIES
indulged, great
bulking
tits, men

come in, doors
open.

NOTE READ re
letter of Lawrence's

to Mrs. Aldous
Huxley? That

films are obscene
if when the young

man and woman come home,
they masturbate one by one.

Not so—
if they make love.

WHAT IS love—
so complete

feet also
are engaged,

nose turns
to look, eyes

find hands,
ears burn—

all a smaller
focus.

I CAN'T
for this variance
wait.

SO SWEET
the body
so expected.

Who comes,
comes
on time.

FOR DAYS neglected
all because he wants to be,
he sits in the afternoon
thinking of love.

Strange body,
grows so vague to him
his head swells
like a lollipop on a stick.

Leave him alone.
He'll remember
when he's hungry
enough.

THE LAST sweet night
of fortune's attitudes.

BRINGING YOU back here—
we were together.

How far away
we were . . .

This distance
is all in one.

SMELLS,
sounds,
pillows.

ALL THE fantasies that
interrupt condition of

sweet union, inex-
orable movement forward.

You haven't
fucked for months now
outside.

Slow slowing—
little
comes of it.

Pretension's
period.

Days in the train, a
sudden *breast*, flatten-
ing model. Walks

with harsh flat
effectiveness past,
and gone forever.

Flesh's
signals—
little
ones.

WHAT'S TO be said.
The bed says nothing.

The place
is many places.

What his idea was,
of no consequence—

hope only
he was one.

ALL THIS flesh, meat,
dreams of eating—

making the water *waves*,
a place to play.

Days go by
uncounted.

Thirty
Things

It is. It is the thing where it is.

WILLIAM CARLOS WILLIAMS
The Descent of Winter

Laughing

Who enters this
kingdom. And
the people
formed in rock.

The Temper

The temper is fragile
as apparently it wants to be,
wind on the ocean, trees
moving in wind and rain.

As You Come

As you come down
the road, it swings
slowly left and the sea
opens below you,
west. It sounds out.

Characteristically

Characteristically and other words,
places of fabulous intent,
mirrors of wisdom, quiet
mirrors of wisdom. Help
the one you think needs it.
Say a prayer to yourself.

•

Echoes preponderantly
backwards. Is alone.

•

I'll dash off
to it.

For Ebbe

And Ebbe
with love.

Surgeons

One imagines a surgeon to be.
The hands move so slowly,
the attention is so steady.

Then one imagines a change,
as if a truck were to leave the highway
and drive up a country road.

Men pick apples for money
in the fall. Surgeons are babies
that grow on trees.

No

No farther out
than in—
no nearer here
than there.

Hey

Hey kid
you.

    •

Flesh filled
to bursting.

As We Sit

There is a long
stretch of sky
before us. The road

goes out to the channel
of the water. Birds
fly in the faintly

white sky. A sound
shuffles over
and over, shifting

sand and
water. A wind
blows steadily

as we sit.

Kitchen

The light in the morning
comes in the front windows,
leaving a lace-like pattern
on the table and floor.

•

In the silence now
of this high square room
the clock's tick adjacent
seems to mark old time.

•

Perpetually sweeping
this room, I want it
to be like it was.

Here

Here is
where there
is.

Echo

Broken heart, you
timeless wonder.

What a small
place to be.

True, true
to life, to life.

Xmas Poem: Bolinas

All around
the snow
don't fall.

Come Christmas
we'll get high
and go find it.

Xmas

It commonly sings,
this Christmas.

But

for Stan's birthday

if we go back to where
we never were we'll
be there. [REPEAT] But

A

head of
the outside
inside.

Photo

for Joanne

They say a
woman passes at
the edge of the
house, turning

the corner, leaves
a very vivid sense,
after her,
of having been there.

Place

Faded mind,
fading colors,
old, dear clothes.
Hear

the ocean under
the road's edge,
down the side
of the hill.

A Loop

No
one
thing

anyone does

For Tom

Friends make
the most of it
the more of it
quite enough.

Post Cards

for Bob Grenier

Each thing,
you didn't even taste it.

•

A red flag
on a red pole.

•

Heaven must spell something.

•

If the telephone rings,
don't say anything.

•

A beating around
the bush. Green
growth.

•

Dad's mother's
death.

•

Up on the top the
space goes further than
the eye can see. We're
up here, calling
over the hill.

In the Fall

The money is cheap
in the fall
by the river
in the woods.

Hanging leaves
hang on, red, yellow,
the wind is sharp,
distances increase.

Still

Still the same
day?
Tomorrow.

Two

Light weighs
light, to the hand,
to the eye.

Feel it
in two places.

Alice

The apple in
her eye.

Change

for Ted

Turning
one wants it all—
no
defenses.

Home

Patsy's
brother
Bill—

Meg's
mother—
Father's

home.
Sweet
home.

One Day

One day after another—
perfect.
They all fit.

Master of All

Master of all things,
wisdom's fine ending
in the air begun with,
water, land's place

in it. Days have gone by
as I have been here.
These things are not
without an ending—

abstract clock
literally so ticks
and I hear it
and look at it.

Hand in the way
of eye's seeing
follows thinking
where to end.

Colors

Colors of stars,
all you people. Cars,
lights, wet streets.

Backwards

Place

There was a path
through the field
down to the river,

from the house
a walk of
a half an hour.

Like that—
walking,
still,

to go swimming,
but only
if someone's there.

Thinking

The top of the mountain
is a pinnacle,
the bottom of the lake

a bed. Sleep fades deep,
floats off as clouds
shift sight to distance, far away.

Here

for Peter

Little earth, water
walking on, sun
singing what's

to come. A
spell, a song,
things seeing,

stone? Or any
one, here, listens,
hears, as one.

Think

Tell the story
'fore your mind goes—
voice coming back in faded tatters.

Backwards

Nowhere before you
any of this.

Time

What happened to her
and what happened to her
and what happened to her?

For the Graduation

Bolinas, 1973

The honor
of being human
will stay constant.

The earth, earth,
water wet, sun
shine.

The world will be
as ever round, and
all yourselves

will know it,
on it, and around
and around.

No one knows
what will
happen. That

is the happiness
of the circle,
finding you.

Flesh

Awful rushes at times
floating out in that emptiness
don't answer nothing for no one.

Seeing dear flesh float by—
days emptied of sun and wind,
hold on to trees and dirt.

Want it under me, body,
want legs to keep working—
don't think anymore of it.

Your face passes down the street—
your hair that was so lovely,
your body, won't wait for me.

Oh Mabel

Oh Mabel, we
will never walk
again the streets

we walked in
1884, my love,
my love.

But You

Sitting next to you
was a place you thought
she was, he was,

sitting next to you
a sense of something
alike, but you,

but you.

Spring

These are the places
one is in, water's
trickling forms, wet

limbs of dripping
trees. Rock pushes
up in springtime, gentle

earth turns wet and
black. This morning was
too late, too late, too late.

Wanting You

Specific light,
water, ground
it's on—heart's

the hard
thing
to define.

Anywhere

Slight wander of innocence
flickers in this wavering
echo of what it had come for,
gone to, and forgotten.

Away

One can own a mirror; does one then own the reflection that can be seen in it?

LUDWIG WITTGENSTEIN
Zettel

Away

for Bobbie

Yourself walked in the room tonight
and it wasn't you. Your way of
being here isn't another's way.
It's all the same somewhere maybe,
and the same old thing isn't you.
All the negatives in existence
don't change anything anyway.

  •

The people tell me a sad story sometimes,
and I tend to tell it back to them.

  •

Come home. It's where you are anyway.
Anyway I wish you weren't home.
Where is home anyway without me.

  •

This place could be rolled up
and put away. Somebody
could warn the so-called people.

I wish I could talk to the people
without going away. Home,
wherever, is where the heart is.

I don't want to talk to the people,
where the heart is. It's home
you and me talk for hours.

  •

For hours I didn't think of you
and then I did and can't stop.

  •

Your birthday is here
without you, that day
you were born to be here.

The loveliest day I saw you
buying your first car
with such a lovely presence, of mind.

It doesn't work without you.
I do, it doesn't. Funny
or not, it's no good.

I'll be home, all ways—
you name it. I'll put a ribbon
on it. You're my love.

    •

Cross in my mind, wanting,
waiting, to get home again.
A kind of weird road
stuck in the middle.

Whatever else it is,
love is the middle
with you and me
right in the middle.

The middle of midnight
is what time it is,
two hours earlier than you,
and me going nowhere.

Only the same time,
your birthday. You and me
at the same time in
the same place, always.

Every Day

Every day
in a little way
things are done.

Every morning there is
a day. Every day
there is a day.

Waking up in a bed
with a window with light,
with a place in mind,

to piss, to eat,
to think of something,
to forget it all,

to remember everything,
perfectly, each
specific, actual detail,

knowing nothing,
having no sense of any of it,
not being a part of it,

all right for you,
all right, you guys—
echoes, things, faces.

Sound

Hearing a car pass—
that insistent distance
from here to there,
sitting here.

Sunlight
shines through the green leaves,
patterns of light and dark,
shimmering.

But so quiet
now the car's gone,
sounds of myself smoking,
my hand writing.

Here

No one
else in the room
except you.

•

Mind's a form
of taking
it all.

•

And the room
opens
and closes.

1971

The year the head
went out into a
field and hid
there. The year
the water came
higher than the edges—

all the people,
all the ways of
getting here and
now, here and
now here.

Berlin: First Night
& Early Morning

I've lost place,
coming here.
The space's noises,

trucks outside, cars
shifting, voices I
can't understand the

words of—how
long ago all this
was otherwise? Tired,

time lost, the room's
narrow size, patience
to be here useless.

All done
long ago, all
gone now.

    •

Cough's explicit
continuity. Little
birds twitter.

    •

The key has a
big metal thing attached
to it, flattened, then

becoming a ball
at one end, with
a rubber washer around it.

    •

Six thirty now.
Air France.

    •

Tame. Marlboro.
Comb and ticket.

•

Not me only
without you—

•

Oh so nice
to be awake
after no sleep
all night.

•

Last night, walking,
the street was slabs
of wild color, signs,
so much to bring to mind.

Things to sell, a long
horizontal of store fronts,
cars, radios, books, and food.
Clothes—people walking too.

•

Absence makes
the heart break
a little bit
wanting out.

•

You: "too abstract,
try it,
all,
over again . . ."

•

Money's got
stylized eagle
on it and a cold
looking man with bald head.

I had to put
on my glasses to
make out its value
while they waited.

They live here,
these people.
Kontakt Linsen,
Abel Optik.

Let us *tanzen*
miteinander
and make love
to *dem Mond*.

For My Mother:
Genevieve Jules Creeley
April 8, 1887–October 7, 1972

Tender, semi-
articulate flickers
of your

presence, all
those years
past

now, eighty-
five, impossible to
count them

one by one, like
addition, sub-
traction, missing

not one. The last
curled up, in
on yourself,

position you take
in the bed, hair
wisped up

on your head, a
top knot, body
skeletal, eyes

closed against,
it must be,
further disturbance—

breathing a skim
of time, lightly
kicks the intervals—

days, days and
years of it,
work, changes,

sweet flesh caught
at the edges,
dignity's faded

dilemma. It
is *your* life, oh
no one's

forgotten anything
ever. They want
to make you

happy when
they remember. Walk
a little, get

up, now, die
safely,
easily, into

singleness, too
tired with it
to keep

on and on.
Waves break at
the darkness

under the road, sounds
in the faint
night's softness. Look

at them, catching
the light, white
edge as they turn—

always again
and again. Dead
one, two,

three hours—
all these minutes
pass. Is it,

was it, ever
you alone
again, how

long you kept
at it, your
pride, your

lovely, confusing
discretion. Mother, I
love you—for

whatever that
means,
meant—more

than I know, body
gave me my
own, generous,

inexorable place
of you. I feel
the mouth's sluggish-

ness, slips on
turns of things
said, to you,

too soon, too late,
wants to
go back to beginning,

smells of the hospital
room, the doctor
she responds

to now, the
order—get me
there. "Death's

let you out—"
comes true,
this, that,

endlessly circular
life, and we
came back

to see you one
last
time, this

time? Your head
shuddered,
it seemed, your

eyes wanted,
I thought,
to see

who it was.
I am here,
and will follow.

Funny

Raining here
in little pieces
of rain.
Wet, brother,

behind the ears,
I love your hands.
And you too,
rain.

You insist on rain
because you are
no less than water,
no more than wet.

Out

Let me walk to you
backwards
down a long street.

.

Here is the rain again.
I hear it
in my ear here.

.

What fun
to be done
if not already
done.

.

We were going
out.

Here Again

After we
were all
a bed,
a door, two
windows
and a chair.

The Plan Is the Body

The plan is the body.
There is each moment a pattern.
There is each time something
for everyone.

The plan is the body.
The mind is in the head.
It's a moment in time,
an instant, second.

The rhythm of one
and one, and one, and one.
The two, the three.
The plan is *in* the body.

Hold it an instant,
in the mind—hold it.
What was said you
said. The two, the three,

times in the body,
hands, feet, you remember—
I, I remember, I
speak it, speak it.

The plan is the body.
Times you didn't want to,
times you can't think
you want to, *you*.

Me, *me*, remember, me
here, me wants to, *me*
am thinking of *you*.
The plan is the body.

The plan is the body.
The sky is the sky.
The mother, the father—
the plan is the body.

Who can read it.
Plan is the body. The mind
is the plan. *I*—
speaking. The memory

gathers like memory, plan,
I thought to remember,
thinking again, thinking.
The mind is the plan of the mind.

The plan is the body.
The plan is the body.
The plan is the body.
The plan is the body.

Blue

Ice not
wet not
hot not
white.

Ice cold.

Dear Dorothy

for Dorothy Dean

Dear Dorothy,
I thought a lot
of what you said—
the gentle art of being nice—

For finks—for you,
"just let me out—
fuck off, you creeps!"
I'd like to get it right

for once, not spend all
fucking life in patience.
I get scared of getting
lost, I hold on hard

to you. Your voice was
instantly familiar. My middle
agéd hippy number
is more words. I like

the tone and place.
I like to drink
and talk to people,
all the lovely faces.

But in the car I'm driving
back to some place on
West Broadway, a man is making
faces at me through the window—

scared, confused at why he
wants to do that. *Why* the
constant pain. It always
hurts—hence drive away

from him. Or, drinking,
go into the men's room,

then come out to
indescribable horrors, lights,

and people *eating* people,
awful. Sounds and noises,
horror, scream at
"what's the matter?" *don't*

you *ever* touch me—
wanting love so much.
Can shake for hours with
thinking, scared it's all got lost . . .

"Would you *fuck* that?"
"My God!" Your ineluctable
smile, it falls back in your head,
you *smile* with such a gentle

giving up. I sadly loved
it that you wopped me with your purse.
"Stupid!" I think of things,
I'm loyal. Narcissist, I want.

Than I

I'm telling you a
story to let myself
think about it. All

day I've been
here, and yesterday.
The months, years,

enclose me as
this thing with arms
and legs. And if

it *is* time
to talk about it,
who knows better

than I?

Comfort

Staggering, you know
they fall
forward to

their desire. Garbage,
pain, people,

want it all,
their comfort
every time.

Dreams

Tunneling through the earth
this way, I didn't know

the surface was where
I had come from. Dreams.

Shot

The bubble breaking
of reflecting mirrors.
Water.

Falling

Falling
from grace—
umpteenth time
rain's hit my head,
generous water.

Sleep

Matrix of your legs,
charming woman,
handholds of firm

proportion—flesh figures in
the signs. Days away
from said past,

backwards "is no
direction"? Thought once,
twice—woke in night

several times as the furniture,
in the dream, backed out
the door, carried by affable

frightening people. Son-
in-law was depressed,
sitting on bed, daughter

beside him—how
had I misunderstood? Me
saying, "no, I

didn't"—little murmur
of self-content? Am
fearful, following

the couch, they have it,
into room occupied by
gang. Hence wake up

without you, bed warm,
sky grey, the day now
to come.

Circle

As from afar,
through ringlet of woods,
the huntsman stares in wonder

at the sight, delight
in that light haze of circle
seems to surround you.

     •

Crashing sound, the woods
move. Leaves fluttering,
birds making chatter—
your body sans error.

     •

Pounds the musculature
where flesh joins bone—
hangs loose, thus
relieves.

Several melding persons,
one face, one
mirror in which to see it?

     •

Expanse of trees
going up block
the light coming down
to us sitting here.

     •

Rolls in laughter,
black hair, generous
action of your body.

     •

Woods all over the place,
find them forever

apparently
where you are.

     •

Isolated,
to think
of you, of you—

sea's plunging forms
and sounds, rock
face, the white, recurring

edge of foam—
love's forms
are various.

     •

In the circle of this
various woods,
one presence, persistent,

shines. An easy seeming
extension of her light
continually brings me to her.

     •

EASE

A day's
pattern
broken,
by your love.

     •

Come here
(come home)
to think

of you
(of you).

     •

A bird
for you, a singing
bird.

•

I'd climb into
your body
if I could, cover

myself up entirely
in your generous
darkening body,

steal away all
senses, sleep
in the hole.

•

You, you, you—
one and only.

•

What use love—
to make me cry,
to make me laugh?

•

Flood of details, memory's
delight—the sight
of you.

•

Waves rolling over,
continuously, sound
of much being done.

Get up, for actions—
impedes the sight, hearing,
—want to walk away?

Stay here. Where I am,
is alone here, on the sand.
Water out in front of me

crashes on.

•

"What are you doing?"
Writing some stuff.

"You a poet?"
Now and then.

•

Woods, water,
all you
are.

•

And the particular
warmth of you,
all asleep
together.

•

WATER

As much to know you,
love, to witness this changing surface
from so constant a place.

•

I'll never get it right enough,
will never stop trying.

•

Old one-eye,
fish head,
wants his water back.

Dear friend,
bring bucket
and shovel.

•

Truly see you,
surfacing, all

slippery, wetness,
at home.

> •

If I wanted
to know myself,
I'd look at you.

When I loved
what I was,
it was that reflection.

> •

Color so changing here,
sky lightens, water

greens, blues.
Never far from you,

no true elsewhere.
My hands stay with me.

> •

You'd think the years
would change some first sense

of whatever it is—
but it comes again and again.

> •

Love's watery condition
waits only for you.

Perfection of substance
leaps high in lacy foam.

Deep as it goes,
entirely you.

> •

Wind gets chill,
sun trying to shine.
Move on again.

In the world a few
things to think of,
a blessing.

I don't love
to prove it—love
to know it.

Bixby Canyon, July 10, 1973

For a Bus on Its Side
and the Man Inside It

Wise house, and
man to know it,

thinks with nothing
farther than arm's reach,

the room of space,
the place of body's

home, ground, grass,
trees, sky, water's

distance, books, all
one in this clear place.

For Walter Chappell

Dream: pigeon—
rooftop, water,
car window

open, crashes in,
get it back there.
The race, against time?

What matter.
Wander with
skin and hands

on my back, my
head, my eye,
tired of ways to get by.

Flying by, flying
off, the roof,
whirls of air,

light sequences, that
setting sun, rock,
stubbed toe against,

I held to, sunk
under it, way
down, such roots

as rocks and trees,
the wind, seem
wise to.

Loving days, loving
eyes, loving
you, loving

ways of loving.
*What's here is
elsewhere, nothing's*

not—don't worry, I
see. See it all
now, open

head surf crashes
through. And
lovely light attentive,

dripping fissures,
all the world,
the world.

If in or out
of it, your friendship
saw the eye

we swam in, brother—
deep ditch with children,
warm nights with water,

sweetening, silver light
become the place
we came to.

"There . . ."

There is a world
underneath, or
on top of,
this one—and
it's here, now.

Easter

Don't
ever refuse
the

people
in their
place.

Phone

What the words,
abstracted, tell:
specific agony,

pain of one so
close, so distant—
abstract here—

Call back, call
to her—smiling voice.
Say, it's all right.

Sick

Belly's full
of rubble.

Sitting Here

for Kate

Roof's peak is eye,
sky's grey, tree's
a stack of lines,

wires across it. This
is window, this is
sitting at the table,

thinking of you,
far away,
whose face is

by the mirror on the bureau.
I love you, I said,
because I wanted to,

because I know you,
my daughter, my
daughter.

I don't want you
to walk away. I
get scared

in this loneliness.
Be *me* again
being born, be the little

wise one walks
quietly by, in the sun,
smiles silently,

grows taller and taller.
Because all these things
passing, changing,

all the things
coming and going
inside, outside—

I can't hold them,
I want to but
keep on losing them.

As if to catch your hand, then,
your fingers, to hang on,
as if to feel

it's all right here
and will be, that
world *is* wonder,

being simply beyond us,
patience its savor,
and to keep moving,

we love what we love,
what we have,
what we have to.

I don't know—
this fact of time spinning,
days, weeks, months, years,

stuffed in some attic.
Or—where can we run,
why do I want to?

As if that touch of you
had, unknowing,
turned me around again

truly to face you,
and your face is wet,
blurred, with tears—

or is it simply years later,
sitting here, and whatever
we were has gone.

Up in the Air

Trees
breathing
air.

•

No longer
closely here
no longer.

•

Fire still burning
in heart. People
move in the oak brush.
Day widens,
music in the room.
Think it's back
where you left it?
Think, think
of nothing.

•

Mind tremors,
(taught) taut rubber,
shimmers of bounce.

•

Sensual body,
a taut skin?

Not the same
mistake "twice"?

Reechoes, re-
collects.

•

Each one
its own imagination

"at best"

This
can be thought of?

of

•

Tree tops
your head

•

"That's very frequent in French."

•

Indignity
no name

•

Those old hotels.

•

"I'm going to take a trip
in that old gospel ship

"I'm going far beyond the sky

—"bid this world goodbye"

"I can scarcely wait . . .
I'll spend my time in prayer—"

"And go sailing through
            the air . . ."

If you are ashamed of me,
you ought not to be . . .

You will sure be left behind,
while *I'm* sailing through

            the air . . .

•

Beauty's desire shall be endless
and a hell of a lot of fun.

•

Luck?
Looks like.

•

Falls
always.

•

You go
that way.
I'll
go this.

•

Many times broke
but never poor.
Many times poor
but never broke.

•

Be welcome
to it.

•

Mind-
ful of feeling,

thinking it.

•

Sun's hand's shadow.
Air passes. Friends.

•

The right one.
The wrong one.
The other one.

•

Heavy time moves
imponderably present.

•

Let her
sing it
for herself.

    •

Keep a distance
recovers space.

San Cristobal, N.M.
May 29, 1974

Uncollected
Poems

Again

I wanted you
without virtue—
so to speak, a history
of alternatives.

Lusts of mind ache
for realization
no less than any appetite
wants enough.

1967

Hero

The boy
with the
finger in
the hole
of the
dike in
Holland.

·

A true story.

·

Here—.

·

This
is it.

1969

As Now It Would Be Snow

1

As now it would be snow
one would see, and in
the days, ways of looking
become as soft as shapes
under the snow, as dumb,
and the trees grey, in
the white light, he said:

the mind is right to
fight the cold for the
cold is not its cold, and
the sun is cold, the
nights as white as days,
against the mind, trying
to put the mind away.

2

As now it would be snow,
he could see the days
become another way which
he could not go back
to, and seeing trees
as sharp, still, in his
mind, he said: the mind is

right. The snow will go
and mind remain, and mind
as cold as snow upon the
shapes of trees, to see
the trees as shapes as
sharp as cold, when sun
has put the snow away.

3

As now it would be snow
he would see, and the
trees no longer sharp
but soft shapes, and for
the eye, a grey against
white, he thought, he
said: the time is right,

and the season cajoled,
and peaceful, what is
to do, is done in the
coldness of the cold
sun, and in a night as
light, as white as day,
I put the mind away.

1970

Sunset

The world
you know as
one piece after
another,

bending its
place in your mind,
looking after the golden
sun.

1972

Places

When I wake next
to you, those moments
are filled with

a warm security,
moist, nuzzling, all
that tenderness

can describe. It
may be simply that
bodies can accomplish

this wonder and where
or whyfor is not
in any way the question.

My head relaxed,
my mind letting go
its assumptions,

weighs the possibility
of sleep or
waking, either one.

In this dearest
half-world all that
confused me otherwise

is absent, nothing
to know or to
explain. You too

are sleeping, your leg
pushes, your arm
falls over my side, you

move with a heavy
surety in the place
your body thus is.

Don't you know this,
I want to shout, you
betrayer—my

ugliness pours poison
out in frustration,
as rage but

also a vaguely
bland quiet, a
reasonable adjustment

to my intent.
I love you and it
gives me grounds

for resentment! I
can see no one
more dear,

and I kill
the desire with
ugly words.

No
longer to
love or

be loved, which
was ever
the question? One

man, only one,
enough to
be *here*, this

place he
finds himself
alone.

1972

Days and Days

HERE AGAIN

After we
were all
a bed,
a door, two
windows
and a chair.

HYPHENS

There is always
someplace.

ONE

Three to the one
makes two.

THOUGHTS

Am I dying?
I am beautiful.
Either way.

NEW YORK

I've just been in New York.
What a place.

Terrific.
You bet.

1973

For the Graduation: Bolinas, 1972

for Kate

Round and round
again, and
up and down
again—always

these days do
go by, and
this one is yours
to go by.

This walking on
and on, this
going and coming—
this morning

shines such lovely
light on
all of us.
We're home.

1974

Looking Out

Warmth
is the way
of all flesh.

The *length*
is skin
and bones—
cold feet!

It's all night
long.

1974

Night in NYC

for Angus

Must be almost four,
light rain
in the city,

cars slide past
as walking feet,
my own,

get me on with it
years past now,
same place.

1974

For Arthur Okamura

It's around
the corner,

flickering
lights, colors,

shapes
of the world's

pieces you've
put

together
again.

*It's around
the corner—*

lights you know
better, old friend.

Pleasure's
a pleasure

so simply
sure.

1975

But

You wouldn't
walk alone. That's

foolishness. But
the trees, the

road, are
company. But,

without another,
what's the fact

but one, useless,
seeing itself go by.

1975

Index of Titles
and First Lines

Index of Titles and First Lines • 653

Index of Titles and First Lines • 659

Index of Titles and First Lines • 661

Index of Titles and First Lines • 665

Index of Titles and First Lines • 669